T0339010

OXFORD HISTORICAL SOCIETY

General Editor: Alan Crossley

MEMOIRS OF THE CITY
AND UNIVERSITY OF OXFORD IN 1738

Oxford Historical Society
NEW SERIES, VOL. XLVII

MEMOIRS OF THE CITY

AND

UNIVERSITY OF OXFORD IN 1738

TOGETHER WITH POEMS, ODD LINES,
FRAGMENTS AND SMALL SCRAPS

by

'SHEPILINDA'
(ELIZABETH SHEPPARD)

Edited with an introduction by

GEOFFREY NEATE

THE BOYDELL PRESS

OXFORD HISTORICAL SOCIETY

MMXVIII

© The Oxford Historical Society 2018

All rights reserved. Except as permitted undcr current legislation
no part of this work may be photocopied, stored in a retrieval system,
published, performed in public, adapted, broadcast,
transmitted, recorded or reproduced in any form or by any means,
without the prior permission of the copyright owner

First published 2018

An Oxford Historical Society publication
Published by Boydell & Brewer Ltd
P0 Box 9, Woodbridge, Suffolk IP12 3DF, UK
and Boydell & Brewer Inc.
668 Mt Hope Avenue, Rochester, NY 14620-2731, USA
website: www.boydellandbrewer.com

ISBN 978-0-904107-29-6

A CIP catalogue record for this book is available
from the British Library

The publisher has no responsibility for the continued existence
or accuracy of URLs for external or third-party internet websites
referred to in this book, and does not guarantee that any content on
such websites is, or will remain, accurate or appropriate

This publication is printed on acid-free paper

Typeset in Monotype Bembo Book by Word and Page, Chester, UK

Printed and bound in Great Britain by
TJ International Ltd, Padstow, Cornwall

CONTENTS

ACKNOWLEDGEMENTS

I am grateful to the Bodleian Library and to Dr. C. J. Y. Fletcher, Keeper of Special Collections, for permission to publish the MS., to Dr. William Poole, Fellow Librarian of New College, for encouraging and assisting the enterprise, and to Theo Dunnet who supplied the initial impetus to publication and introduced me to Dr. Poole. It is also a pleasure to thank all the archivists who supplied comments elucidating the Shepilinda passages relating to their colleges. I owe a special debt to my editor Alan Crossley, who has guided this edition from its early stages to publication with care, good advice, and good humour. He also compiled the Index.

ABBREVIATIONS

ODNB	*Oxford Dictionary of National Biography*
OED	*Oxford English Dictionary*
OHC	Oxfordshire History Centre, Oxford
OHS	Oxford Historical Society
VCH	*Victoria County History*

INTRODUCTION

Shepilinda's *Memoirs & Poems* is a light-hearted but invaluable eighteenth-century document composed by an engaging writer which has not received the attention it deserves. It is a first-hand account of the Oxford colleges in 1738 written by a young woman calling herself 'Shepilinda', who, it seems, had a measure of social access to many of them. She was accompanied by a friend and confidante with the nickname 'Scrippy' for whom the resulting memoir and appended collection of poems are intended as a gift. She clearly had a facility for getting people to talk to her quite freely, together with a quick grasp of the information she received. She also had a lively, sometimes mischievous, sense of humour.

The value of the document for us, other than the pleasure it gives us to read it, is that it records a number of otherwise unknown facts[1] and personalities.[2]

THE MANUSCRIPT

Bodleian Library manuscript MS. Top. Oxon. d 287 comprises 82 paper leaves guarded and bound between solid utilitarian mauve covers with external dimensions W 17.7 cm. x H 20.5 cm. The leaves have been numbered in pencil at top right as 1–8, 8a, 9–81. On folios 10 to 43r the pages have also been numbered in ink at top outside as 1 to 67, while the pages of folios 46 to 53r have been similarly numbered 19 to 33.[3] Folios 54 to 79 are blank except that

---

[1] See e.g. the 'end of all things' (below, p. 55, n. 256).
[2] See e.g. the account of Mrs. Cockman (below, p. 26, n. 106). Women in the colleges are hardly mentioned in other eighteenth-century sources.
[3] These page numbers have been enclosed in single quotation marks in the edition, e.g. fol. 12r '5', etc.

70 to 75 rectos have traces of written line ends at the left edge[4] and some have been repaired. The damage and repairs continue to folio 78. Since a letter of donation is part of the guarded assemblage the binding (or rebinding) must have been carried out by the Library.

THE TEXT

The MS. consists of five sections, of which two carry titles:

a. (folios 1–8a) Four twentieth-century letters (unmounted) relating to the work contained in the remaining leaves.

b. (folios 9–44) *'Shepilinda's memoirs of the City and University of Oxford. Jan^ry 7th 1737/8. For Dear Scrippy'.*

c. (folios 45–53) *'The 2nd part & End of Sheppy for Scrip Containing Poems odd lines Fragments & Small Scraps May 2nd 1738'.*

d. (folios 54–79) Blank leaves.

e. (folios 80–1) The untitled dedication beginning *'Dedications are generaly at the Beginning of a Book which made me chuse mine at the latter End'.*

The handwriting is confident and reasonably neat at the beginning. It then becomes increasingly untidy with variations in size until the third section (the poems) is reached. Here the need to fit lines within the page width has required a smaller hand, which is sometimes difficult to make out. Punctuation is very sparse throughout. Spelling is often haphazard even for the period. (The author sometimes forgets and sometimes corrects the spelling of 'Principal' meaning Head of House.) She shows a distinct tendency to write 'oi' following 'v' where 'io' is required: *voilent* (fol. 46v), *Voilet<s>* (fol. 48v), *voil* (fols. 52v, 53r), *Voiloncella* (fol. 53r), which perhaps indicates a slight rusticity in her speech but the language is educated and the style accomplished.

---

4   These line ends are fragmentary and appear to be the result of inaccurate cutting or folding at the time of binding. Those on fol. 74r complete the lines of fol. 15v (see below, p. 14, n. 58).

There are some instances of attempted total erasure of words or phrases, which, together with at least one of the interlinear additions (fol. 40r), are probably not by the author.

MODERN HISTORY OF THE MANUSCRIPT

The existence of the manuscript was first communicated in print by John Richard Magrath, Provost of Queen's, in 1904. In his edition of the correspondence of Daniel and others of the Fleming family and their acquaintances in the years 1650 to 1700 he has a source note to his description of the practice at Queen's of poorer students waiting at table (Magrath 1904, p. 556 additional note 235, 5). The source note reads: 'The practice continued for at least sixty years after this, as in 'Shepilinda's Memoirs,' a MS. belonging to the Revd. Egerton Leigh, Vicar of Kirkstall, Yorkshire, dated 7 Jan. 1737/8 we read: 'the Fellows that dine at the high Table Sit at the High Table sit all with their backs against the Wall, & the poor Tabiters that wait upon them, Stand with their Faces towards them, & their thumbs across upon the table; which custom has been ever since one of them Stab'd a person in the time of Diner or Super, I don't know which, but my Memory won't let me tell you, who it was, how it was, nor when it was, but thus much I believe that true it was' (Magrath 1904, pp. 556ff.).

More of the contents were revealed by A. D. Godley in 1908. He wrote (Godley 1908, p. vi): 'I am under a special obligation to the Provost of Queen's College, who has allowed me to see a MS. *Memoir* which throws some light on Oxford Society', and later gives a number of short quotations in which he reveals that the author called herself 'Shepilinda' (pp. 65, 91, 136, 196, 252). The manuscript is clearly on loan to Magrath,[5] and in his 1921 history of his

---

[5] See Magrath's letter dated 1930 in Appendix A (Letter 4): 'I have had it by me more than 25 years.'

College he quotes from Shepilinda's account. He explains in a footnote that '*Shepilinda's Memoirs of the City and University of Oxford, Jany 7th, 1737–8* is a Satirical account of the University and Colleges written by, or in the character of, a young lady of the period', and expresses the hope that 'it may, after the war, be printed in the next volume of Collectanea, for the Oxford Historical Society'[6] (Magrath 1921, vol. 2, p. 97, n. 1). These words were obviously written some years before the actual appearance of his book, and Magrath had in fact taken steps towards publication but was unsuccessful (see the discussion of the First Transcript below).

Of the four letters included at the front of the volume[7] the first is from the owner, the Revd. Neville Egerton Leigh of Kirkstall Vicarage, Leeds. The fourth is from Magrath to Bodley's Librarian Arthur Cowley donating the volume to the Library with the explanation that this had been the wish of the owner (who had died the previous year). The other two are covering letters from persons returning the manuscript after borrowing it, one expressing the view that it is not worth publishing in full, the other hoping that it will be.

IDENTITY OF THE AUTHOR

When P. S. Spokes[8] catalogued the manuscript in 1964 he was able to dispel the doubts about the author's name: 'The authoress, as appears from references on fols. 10, 40,

---

6   In the letter quoted below, p. xxviii, n. 58. Salter goes on: 'One hardly knows whether a volume will be needed next year …'.

7   See Appendix A.

8   Peter Spencer Spokes (1893–1976) local historian, bibliographer, archaeologist, conservationist, and city councillor. (He was Lord Mayor of Oxford 1968/9.) He worked in the Bodleian as Extra Staff in the Department of Western Manuscripts for over 25 years until his death (*Bodleian Library Staff Newsletter* 415, 30 Jan. 1976). His daughter Ann Spokes Symonds has produced the first volume of 'The life of Peter Spencer Spokes' (1996), which covers the period up to 1939 and includes tributes in an Epilogue.

43, was Elizabeth, daughter of William Sheppard of Hart Hall.'[9] The internal evidence he adduced was indeed clear enough. Folio 10r mentions 'Black Bess (my Namesake)' and folio 43r includes, in a description of 'Frog Hall', 'The Principal is William Sheppard Esqr. ... the Principal has a Wife & one Daughter (that's me).' The description of Hart Hall at fol. 40r includes the statement 'my pappa was bred up a Gentleman Commoner here'.

'Shepilinda' is, therefore, the pseudonym of Elizabeth Sheppard. Her father William Sheppard had attended Hart Hall and accordingly has an entry in Foster, *Alumni*. It runs: 'Sheppard. William, s. Rob., of Woodstock, Oxon., equitis. HART HALL, matric. 12 Mar. 1704/5, aged 17.' Robert has his own entry as Sir Robert Sheppard of Great Rollright, Oxon., armiger, having matriculated from Corpus Christi on 12 Feb. 1684/5 aged 18, and is named as son of William Sheppard, gent., who matriculated from St. John's College on 13 November 1650. William's father, also called William, is not recorded as having attended the University but was admitted to Lincoln's Inn in 1629, being named as the son of yet another William.[10]

The Sheppards of Great Rollright were a well-to-do Oxfordshire family. The most famous member was Elizabeth's great-great-uncle Sir Fleetwood Sheppard, a rakish Restoration character who became Nell Gwyn's chamberlain.[11] His name was given to Elizabeth's young brother who died and has been perpetuated in the family into modern times.[12]

---

[9] Spokes 1964, p. 75.

[10] '1629 Oct 12 WILLIAM SHEPPARD, son and heir app. of Wm. S., late of Gt. Rowlwright, Oxon., arm., decd., special admission': *Records of the Honorable Society of Lincoln's Inn, Vol. I, Admissions from A.D. 1420 to A.D. 1799* (Lincoln's Inn, 1896, p. 209).

[11] See Foster, *Alumni* and *ODNB*.

[12] In direct descent there are Elizabeth's great-grandson Fleetwood Thomas Hugh Wilson (b. 1817) and his son Guy Douglas Arthur Fleetwood Wilson (1851–1940). In the Sheppard line we have the Revd. Henry Fleetwood Sheppard (1824–1901), who was co-author with Sabine Baring Gould of *Songs and Ballads*

We note that when William matriculated in 1705 his father is recorded as living at Woodstock rather than Great Rollright. If this reflects business interests they may have shifted to Oxford a few years later although the family location is once more Great Rollright. Oxford Council Acts have the following entry for 8 Sept. 1710: 'Mr. Robert Sheppard of Rollright is to be admitted free[13] and have a bailiff's place, he giving the usual treat for the occasion.'[14] The editor notes that 'William' is written in the margin of the original document. Robert was 43 and William was 22; perhaps the father decided to cede the bailiff's place to his son from the outset.[15]

ELIZABETH SHEPPARD

Elizabeth Sheppard was born in Great Rollright on 29 September 1713, the daughter and first child of William and Ann Sheppard.[16] Her father was the son of Robert Sheppard of Great Rollright, Oxfordshire, and Ann Greswolde of Malvern Hall, Warwickshire, while her mother was the daughter of Thomas Doley of Olton End, Warwickshire, and Elizabeth Palmer,[17] also of Olton End; all four were seemingly prosperous families.[18] Elizabeth's parents' prior-

of the West: A Collection Made from the Mouths of the people. Harmonised and arranged for voice and pianoforte by H. Fleetwood Sheppard (London, Methuen 1891).

[13] Robert would not be allowed to transact business in Oxford unless he were first made a freeman.

[14] For the purchase of bailiff's places, see Fasnacht 1954, p. 131; _VCH Oxon._ iv. 136.

[15] Hobson 1954, p. 62. It is not clear whether Robert's title was mistakenly or deliberately ignored.

[16] Great Rollright baptismal register: 'Elizabeth ye daughter of William Sheppard and Ann Born Sep 29 1713'.

[17] Elizabeth Sheppard was almost certainly named after her Doley grandmother (1652–1720). See the inscription on the memorial tablet placed by Ann in the Church of St. Alphege, Solihull, 'to perpetuate the pious memory of the best of mothers' (Pemberton 1905, p. 174). The name would also be in memory of Ann's sister Elizabeth who died in 1705 aged twelve (Pemberton 1905, p. 43).

[18] Especially, perhaps, the Palmers: see p. xviii with n. 31.

ity must have been to produce a male heir to the family name but two diamond-figure memorial slabs in the bell tower floor of St. Andrew's parish church at Great Roll-right testify to the tragedy of their failure: Jane and Fleetwood both died in infancy.[19] One assumes that their hopes turned instead to ensuring a good match for Elizabeth and that was the reason for moving to Oxford, probably on 29 November 1736 (when she was 23) if we accept that this is what lies behind Elizabeth's tendentious date for the revival of 'Frog Hall' (below, p. 63).

It must be that every influence and expenditure were used to offer Elizabeth an *entrée* to all the colleges. Given her sparky personality and acute powers of intelligent observation the plan was a good one, and she herself knew what she was about: in the *Memoirs* she archly emphasizes the bachelor status of any unmarried College Head. (Generally the head of house was the only Fellow allowed to marry and keep his position.)

The poem 'The following wrote upon somebody' (below, p. 84) may hint that at least one candidate for marriage was vetoed by Elizabeth's parents but nothing more is known about her stay in Oxford after the Memoirs cease. The bare facts concerning the remainder of her life after she left the city are that she married, bore one child, and died. Dates have not yet been found but Burke's *Landed gentry*, Pemberton's *Solihull and its church*, and the Wilson family tradition record the marriage of Elizabeth Sheppard to the Revd. William Harries, son of George Harries, of Granston, Pembrokeshire. William Harries appears in Foster, *Alumni* (cross-referenced to Harris) as 'Harris, William, s. George, of Grandston [i.e. Granston], co. Pembroke,

---

[19] 'Here lies the body of Iane youngest daughter of WILLIAM SHEPPARD Esq. and of ANNE his wife who died the 12th of April 1723 in yᵉ 9. Yʳ. of her Age'. The other memorial is largely worn away: '[Here lies the body of] FLEETWOOD son of WILLIAM SHEPPARD Esq. [and of ANNE his] wife who was [...] 13 1727 [in yᵉ 1ˢᵗ Yʳ of his Age]'. The parish burials register records 17 April 1723 (Jane) and 9 May 1728 (Fleetwood).

gent. Jesus Coll., matric. 29 Mar. 1737, aged 17; B.A. 1740, M.A. 1743'. Burke has this: 'William Richard Wilson (b. in 1737) married Jane Anne Eleanor, daughter of the Revd. W. Harries of Bryn Hyfrid, co. Pembroke,[20] by Elizabeth his wife, only child of William Sheppard, Esq. of Great Rollwright, Oxfordshire by Anne his wife, only daughter of Thomas Doley, of Olton End, co. Warwick ...'.[21] Pemberton includes the marriage in a tree of important families as 'Elizabeth Sheppard = (Rev.) W. Harries of Bryn Hyfrid, Pemb.' with offspring 'Jane Ann Eleanor Harries, d. 1827, Lady of Knowle Manor' marrying 'Capt. William Richard Wilson, b. 1737, d. c1798'.[22]

William Harries' mother is recorded as Elinor Jones.[23] Jane Ann(e) Eleanor Harries, Elizabeth's only child, was therefore named after both her grandmothers, as well, one guesses, as the aunt who died in infancy. The Revd. William Harries made a second marriage: it was to Elizabeth,[24] daughter of Owen Edwardes, of Treffgarne, but she died (or became incapacitated) in 1747 and there was no issue.[25] He became vicar of St. Dogwells (Pembs.) in 1756 and continued there until 1786, the year before he died. It is possible that he is the Revd. William Harries who in 1760 was elected a member of the Society of Sea Serjeants, a kind of Pembrokeshire dining and holiday club suspected,

---

[20] i.e. Brynhyfryd, in the parish of St. Dogwells, mentioned below.

[21] Burke 1863, p. 1677. The entry is quoted without attribution by Wilson 1922, p. 159 (with further corruption of the toponym to 'Bryn Hyfied').

[22] Pemberton 1905, p. 43 (Table E. Families of Greswold, Lewis, Hawes, Palmer, Wigley, and Williams).

[23] 'George Harries of Tregwynt ... His wife was Elinor, daughter of William Jones of Llether by Jennett his wife': Francis Jones, 'Harries of Tregwynt', in *Cymmrodorion*, Sessions 1943–4 (1946), p. 114. (Tregwynt is the great house at Granston.)

[24] Ibid. p. 115; Mrs C. O. Higgon and F. Green in *West Wales Hist. Rec.*, vol. viii (1921), 201. Burke 1835 (vol. 2, p. 314) by contrast omits the fourth child Jane and names the fifth (who married William Harries) as Ann instead of Elizabeth. Neither source knows of the first marriage to Elizabeth Sheppard.

[25] William was granted administration of his wife's goods in 1747 (Francis Jones, 'Harries of Tregwynt', p. 115).

probably without cause, of being Jacobite activists.[26] It is dangerous to argue from silence but it would appear that he played no part in his daughter's upbringing.

The wills of both Elizabeth's parents are extant and are the best key at present to her last years. Her father William Sheppard wrote his will in 1742[27] and died the same year. In it he names Elizabeth Sheppard (not Harries) as his only daughter and does not say she is married. He makes trust provision for her. Her mother Ann Sheppard wrote her will in 1745[28] and died in 1746: she had been living at Olton End, seat of both her parents' families, since at least 26 October 1743.[29] She does not mention Elizabeth and leaves the bulk of her estate in trust for Jane Ann Eleanor Harris, her granddaughter, until her 21st year or marriage. Some way down the list of bequests she leaves £10 to William Harries, named as her son-in-law, for mourning.

The conclusion is that between 2 May 1738 (the date of the poems) and 12 July 1742 (the date of her father's will) Elizabeth remained unmarried, and that during the period from then until 29 October 1745 (the date of her mother's will) she married William Harries, gave birth to Jane, and died.

ELIZABETH'S DAUGHTER AND IMMEDIATE DESCENDANTS

Elizabeth Sheppard's only child, Jane Ann(e) Eleanor Harries of Brynhyfryd, Pembrokeshire (date of birth

---

[26]   Fenton 1811, pp. 462–8 (Revd. William Harries named on p. 467). For the Society, see also Francis Jones, 'Disaffection and dissent in Pembrokeshire', in *Cymmrodorion*, Sessions, 1946–7 (1948), pp. 221ff.

[27]   OHC, BOR4/49/4/W/5 (Copy of will of William Sheppard of Great Rollright, 12 July 1742).

[28]   Shakespeare Centre Library and Archive, Stratford-upon-Avon, DR 37/2/Box 90/36 (Copy will of Ann Sheppard, Oldton End, Solihull, widow. 29 Oct. 1745).

[29]   Date of conveyance, MS 3100/ACC 1910-006/224615 held by Birmingham City Archives, which names 'Anne Sheppard of Olton End in the parish of Solihull, widow'.

undetermined), married William Richard Wilson (1737–1808), a captain of the 3rd Dragoon Guards, in 1762.[30] He was of the Wilson family of Knowle Hall, Warwickshire, but with branches also in Jordanstone, Pembrokeshire, and in Hafod Wen, Carmarthenshire, and he was born in the last of these places, the son of John Wilson, an army officer, and Elizabeth Williams (Jones 1987, p.91). He and Jane became Lord and Lady of Knowle Hall and had one son, William, born in 1774, who became a vicar in North-amptonshire and continued to live at Knowle Hall (ibid. and Pemberton 1905, p. 43). They also had two daughters who died in infancy (Wilson 1922, p. 159). William married Martha Bowen Jordan of Waterston House, Pembroke-shire, and they had three sons and four daughters (one named 'Elinor'). When Jane Ann(e) Eleanor Wilson died in 1827 William inherited a considerable share of the Palmer fortune,[31] but in 1831 he accidentally shot himself while clambering through a hedge with a loaded gun.[32] The three sons left behind were William Henry Bowen Jordan Wilson (known as 'Gumley' Wilson,[33] 1808–87), John Richard Sheppard Wilson (1812–71), and Fleetwood Thomas Hugh Wilson (1817–62). The fortune went to 'Gumley', who managed to spend it all and ruin himself so that he had to remove to America for some time, and could be no help to his siblings or their children. Nevertheless it is from him that we have our only account of Shepilinda's daughter. His nephew, Guy Fleetwood Wilson (Fleetwood Thomas Hugh's son), persuaded him to set down his memoirs, including the following:

[30]   Pemberton 1905, p. 43.

[31]   As the eldest son he inherited the 'Warwickshire estate, called the Palmer estate' consisting of 'Knowle, Olton and Milverton, close to Leamington ... After the division Knowle and Milverton fell to me, and Olton to Colonel Greswolde': Wilson 1924, p. 30.

[32]   Wilson 1924, pp. 29ff.

[33]   From Gumley near Market Harborough, Leics., where he refurbished the house which became 'Gumley Hall', his home: Wilson 1924, pp. 31ff.

> My grandmother Jordan, of Jordanstone, Carmarthenshire, was the regular old-fashioned 'dame' of the country squire ... My grandmother Wilson was of quite a different style. She was a Herries of Bryn-Hyfrid and Tregwent in Pembrokeshire. She was the thorough gentlewoman of the old school—well read—clever and could talk well on most subjects. She had moved about a good deal with my grandfather in her younger days—mixed in the world, and in the best society, and was a very charming old woman.[34]

He had reason to be grateful to her. He recalls:

> My grandmother Wilson, who lived at London, took possession of me from my birth, that is she paid all expenses of my schooling, clothing, Army commissions and allowance in the Army to the day of her death. She had an income from funds and the Palmer estates of some £3,000 odd per annum, and was in those days a rich woman.[35]

ELIZABETH'S COUSINS AND HER COMPANION

Elizabeth mentions cousins at three points: (1) p. 9 has 'There are many parcels of Building in this College [Balliol] (Couzen Hoby's are the best).' This is the future Sir Philip 5th Baronet Hoby of Marlow, Bucks. (see note 36 below); (2) p. 28, 'I have two Couzons both Gentlemen Commoners of this College [University].' She does not name them but they are Humphrey Greswold (1720–44) and Marshall Greswold (1721–48), the sons of her paternal grandmother's brother the Revd. Marshall Greswold of Malvern Hall (1674–1728) and his wife Martha, née Makepeace. They matriculated together on 8 July 1737; (3) p. 40, 'My Cozen Mill is a Gentleman Comoner of this College [New], his lodgings are pretty & neat; only he wants a Scutching to one of his Cupboard locks, which my Cozen Philadelphia & I pulled of.' This is Richard Mill (1716–66) who would become 6th Baronet Mill, and

---

[34] Wilson 1924, p. 13.
[35] Ibid. pp. 14ff.

Philadelphia was his sister who died unmarried in 1782. Interestingly the Hoby and Mill cousins were to converge: when Sir Philip Hoby ('Cousin Hoby') died without issue in 1766 he bequeathed his estate to John Mill, son of Richard ('Cousin Mill'), provided that he add to his own name the name and arms of Hoby. John then became Sir John Hoby Mill, Bart.[36] It has not been determined whether the Hobys and Mills were related to Elizabeth on her mother's or her father's side.

Shepilinda had as companion on some if not all of her visits the dedicatee of the Manuscript. We know her only by her nickname 'Scrippy' or 'Scrip'; she seems to have had a similar sense of humour, and it is because of her that we have the manuscript and also that it is so fascinating a document, for it is doubtful that Elizabeth Sheppard would have written so wittily if it had been merely for a private journal, or so freely if it had been for a more formal correspondent. At one point (below, p. 50) Shepilinda has '<u>he</u> Scrip and <u>She</u> Scrip, both say so, & they are oracles': this would most naturally refer to a husband.

In her account of University College Shepilinda not only mentions her cousins but also mentions and names a brother: 'there is now a vacancy among the Fellows, for Our Admirable B^r Benvolio alias the Revnd Mr Brown[37] is made ArchDeacon of Northampton' (p. 28). Also, in the poem 'If Scrip c^d imagine how hard 'twas to write'

---

[36] Dallaway 1815, p. 233 (chart).

[37] John Browne (1687–1764) came up to Univ. in 1704 and was made a Browne Exhibitioner in November 1705 and a Freeston minor Exhibitioner in October 1708. He was elected a Skirlaw Fellow in August 1711 and resigned his Fellowship in March 1738/9 after his appointment as Archdeacon of Northampton. He then came back to Univ. in 1745, when he was elected Master to succeed Thomas Cockman, and remained in post until his death in August 1764. See Darwall-Smith 2008, Chapter 12 [RD-S]. Foster *Alumni*: 'Brown, John, s. Richard, of Marton, Yorks, gent. University Coll., subscribed 23 May, 1704, aged 17; B.A. 26 Jan., 1707–8, M.A. 1710, B.D. 1719, D.D. 1745, Master 1744–64, Vice-Chancellor 1750–3, vicar of Aldborough, Yorks, 1723–62, died 7 Aug., 1764'.

(below, p. 82) she refers to: '… Merry King Alfred's Royal Foundation where we had a brother a Civilised Youth'. In fact, Elizabeth had no surviving brother and so the reference must be to Scrippy's sibling. In the first passage he is nicknamed 'Benvolio' but is then named as Rev^nd Mr Browne and is correctly reported as having just been made Archdeacon of Northampton. Although John Browne was to become Master of his college and Vice-Chancellor of the University, next to nothing is known about his life apart from his university and college posts.[38] Whether he had siblings, whether he married or not, these were unanswered questions until now. Shepilinda, it seems, gives him a sister, although we do not have her real forename or her married name. The poem is problematical. It refers to a 'brother', locates him in University College, and finishes '& (we) Both took our leaves of our B^r & friend', i.e. Scrippy's brother and Shepilinda's friend. But the poem also calls him a 'civilised <u>youth</u>', describes him as hopelessly disorganised, and refers to his 'Wife' (underlined), standing in the corner saying nothing (p. 83).[39] Perhaps this is a younger brother of John. Further, we find that Shepilinda's mother includes the clause: 'to Rev. John Brown, Master of University College, Oxon., £20' in her will.[40] He was clearly either a family friend or related by marriage, and this would explain why his sister was selected to be Elizabeth's companion on her visits to the colleges.

John Browne was 50 or 51 years old in 1738, and we are justified in concluding that his sister, even if several years younger, was considerably older than the 24-year-old

---

[38] 'John Browne, however, remains the most obscure eighteenth-century Master of University College. No collection of his papers exists; no diarist or writer of memoirs is known to have alluded to him; and no portrait survives.' Darwall-Smith 2008, p. 267. We are therefore grateful for the meagre information from Hearne that 'his voice was too low' when, as a younger man, he preached at St. Mary's (28 Apr. 1717) vol. 6 (OHS xliii), 8.

[39] The passage is difficult. See below, p. 85 and n.

[40] See above, note 37.

Elizabeth. Although the memoirs and poems show them as laughing and larking together it is likely that Scrippy also functioned, however informally, as a chaperone.

THE CONTENT OF THE MEMOIRS

In these *Memoirs* Shepilinda presents vignettes of the colleges (followed by the halls) in terms of their buildings, their history, their 'curiosities' both inanimate and human, their customs, and any interesting or humorous anecdotes, frequently involving personalities, which appealed to her. The results are not systematic but are often lively, and they sometimes conjure up the picture of the younger college fellows dropping their guard and responding to the vivacity of their interrogator with amusing accounts of the quirks and eccentricities of their society and environment.[41] It cannot be denied that a taste for scandal is occasionally apparent.

At the end of the account of each college, sometimes after a definite statement that she has finished with the college in question,[42] appears a summary in rather dry, guide-book style of the main facts relating to founder and foundation date, the architectural units, and the garden or gardens. The composition of the establishment (Visitor, fellows, commoners, choristers, etc.) may come next, to be rounded off with a statistic not usually found in histories or guides, viz. the length in feet[43] of the college. Only one measurement is given and so the main street frontage is presumably what is meant.[44]

---

[41] At St. John's she and Grace Gardiner have a lively acquaintance with six named fellows. See the poem 'Now you shall hear' on p. 71.

[42] E.g. 'Exeter's done with now' (below, p. 14); 'that's all I have to say of this College' (i.e. Wadham, p. 37).

[43] In three cases the measurement is to the nearest six inches.

[44] No source for these measurements has been found. A few of them include an odd six inches. It seems unlikely that they were Elizabeth's personal pacings.

It is clear from the manuscript that Shepilinda left space, even whole pages, for these factual descriptions to be added after her personal accounts: when she came back to them later on she sometimes wrote in a larger hand to fill out the extra space.[45] If we look for a printed source none has yet been identified.[46] It may be important that Worcester is the only college which lacks such a tail piece; it suggests that her source, if there was a single source, dated from before 1714.

There is a manuscript parallel to her subjoined summaries in Thomas Baskerville's description of the University. Thomas (1630–1700) did not, like his father Hannibal, attend it but he loved it and had a number of friends there.[47] He has left an account of it,[48] written in about 1683 to 1686, which has been published (omitting the most seriously lengthy of his many digressions).[49] Like Shepilinda he describes each of the colleges. Both writers favour summary statements of foundation and establishment data and they can show similarities,[50] e.g. All Souls:

> [Baskerville 1905, p. 192] All Soules Colledge founded in the dayes of Henry Chichley, Archbishop of Canterbury ... All Souls, besides ye present Warden, James, in Diuinitie, hath 40 fellows, 2 Chaplains, 3 Clarks, 6 Choristers, besides other orders.

[45] E.g. Corpus Christi, fol. 25v.

[46] 'It is not from any obvious edition of Chamberlaine's *Angliae Notitia* or Ayliffe's *Antient and Present State of Oxford*, as one might suspect': personal communication from Dr. William Poole.

[47] *ODNB.*

[48] Bodleian MS. Rawlinson D. 810. The quality of his narrative varies alarmingly: near the beginning of the actual account of Oxford he offers the lovely image of the city 'being sweetly hugg'd in ye pleasant Arms of those 2 pure Rivers the Tems & Charwell', but immediately follows it with a silly explanation of its name as originating from a 'Queen in Elder days', pursued by enemies and fleeing on ox-back, crying: 'Ox on!'

[49] Baskerville 1905.

[50] However, Baskerville does not supply measurements except when he reports that Magdalen Cloister is 60 by 51 paces (p. 185) or when he offers various personal pacings of the Botanical Garden (p. 187).

[Shepilinda, below, p. 25] All Souls College was founded in 1437 by Henry Chichely Abp of Canterburry ... it has a Warden 40 Fellows 2 Chaplains 3 Clerks 6 Choiristers &c

and Queen's:

[Baskerville, p. 221] Queens Colledge was built Año 1340, by Robert Eaglesfield ... It hath a Prouost Timothy Halton D^r of Divinity, 14 ffellows, 7 schollars, 2 Chapplains, 14 poor Children besides other orders.

[Shepilinda, below, p. 46] Queens College is beholden for its Name <to> Philippa King Edwd the 2^{nds} Wife; but the real Founder was her Confessor Robt Eglefield. the Society consists of a Provost 14 Fellows 7 exhibitioners 2 chaplains &C

The most striking resonance is in the account of Corpus Christi because there, and only there, does Shepilinda use the archaic 'hath' instead of 'has', and Baskerville had also used it:

[Baskerville, p. 217] Corpus Christi Coll; was built by Rich: Fox, Bishop of Winchester, 1516, one of the Privy Councell to Henry ye 7th & 8th and privy seal. It hath a President, Robert Newling, D^r of Divinity, 20 ffellows, 20 Schollars, 2 Chaplens, besides other orders.

[Shepilinda, below, p. 34] Corpus Christi College Founded AD 1516 By R^d Fox Bp of Winton Privy Councelour & Ld Priv Seal to Henry ye 7th & 8 it hath a President 20 Fellows 20 Scholars & two Chaplains &c.

Baskerville contracted to have his collected writings printed but died (in 1700) before it was done.[51] Richard Rawlinson acquired the account of Oxford at some time in the next fifty-five years, perhaps from the relatives Baskerville had in St. Giles,[52] in which case Shepilinda could have seen

---

[51] *ODNB*: Thomas Baskerville (b. 1630 Sunningwell near Abingdon. Sources differ as to whether he died in 1700 or in 1720). It may be that two members of the family have been conflated.

[52] 'St Giles, where among other gentry who live in that street, my honor'd unkle Paul Dayrel and dame Barbara his wife, my mother's sister, haue a good house ...' (Baskerville 1905, p. 192).

the manuscript before it changed hands. There is also the possibility that there was an intermediate, or even a prior, source unidentified or no longer extant.

The last of the halls Shepilinda treats of is 'Frog Hall': it quickly becomes apparent that this is the abode of the Sheppard family and is unlikely to have borne that name in reality. The descriptions of the colleges and halls are then rounded off with short accounts of three other topics: a brief note on the addition of an upper floor to the Bodleian; a heartfelt complaint about hornblowing practice in preparation for May Day; and a summary of the popular account of the city's annual penance for the St. Scholastica's Day massacre.

THE POEMS

The poems which make up the second and shorter part of the manuscript have much of the same wit and vivacity as the Memoirs. They also show a talent for rhymed verse, whether in a racy account of a trip into the countryside and the attentions of a superannuated suitor, or else in the formal exercise of a pastoral, or again in a description of a music concert with a valuable mention of a few of the solo performers by name.

SHEPILINDA'S SOCIAL ACCESS TO THE COLLEGES

Elizabeth Sheppard and her companion visited most of the colleges and not only saw the relatively accessible gardens and chapels but, in the case of Queen's, watched the senior members at dinner from the gallery and then joined them in the common room where 'Scrip poked the fire for them' (p. 43). At University College the observation that Mrs Cockman was given to 'washing her hands in the middle of dinner' (p. 26) also implies that Shepilinda was present at such a meal. It should be remembered that *dinner* at this period took place at what we would consider to be lunchtime and never in the hours of darkness.[53] There was also a light supper in the late afternoon or early evening: the Queen's passage begins 'the hall where scrip and I saw them dine & once I saw them Sup'.[54] Women could be present in the shape of the wives of Heads of House and possibly the wives of chaplains, given the confusion at Christ Church as to whether they were allowed to marry (p. 51 and note). The presence at dinner in Hall of Miss Wyntle, sister of the (unmarried) Warden of Merton, is not stated but is perhaps implied by Shepilinda's having to listen to her interminable talking (below, p. 30).

Celia Fiennes supplies a precedent for the hospitality shown to Elizabeth Sheppard. On her Oxford visit in about 1694 she visited Corpus Christus [sic] Colledge 'which is but small—there I was entertained at supper, and eate of their very good bread and beare which is remarkably the best any where Oxford Bread is' (Fiennes 1947, p. 34). After Shepilinda's time in September 1774 Mrs Thrale visited Oxford with her husband and Dr. Johnson, and reports: 'we dined in the Hall at University College, where I sat in the seat of honour ... We drank tea in the Common room, had a world of talk, and passed the evening with cheerfulness and comfort' (Darwall-Smith 2008, p. 290).

The lively interaction of Elizabeth Sheppard and Grace Gardiner with the younger Fellows of St. John's (p. 71) might have been in the Common room but could equally well have taken place in the quadrangles and gardens.

---

[53] In the colleges the hour of the meal called *dinner* steadily advanced during the first half of the eighteenth century. It had been ten o'clock in the morning but was early on postponed to eleven. Later in the century it moved on to 3 or 4 p.m. Shepilinda defines the usual times of dinner and supper in 1738 in her comment on pp. 39–40: 'you must know the Fellows [of New College] Bowl here to get them stomachs to relish their 12 & 6 a Clock Comons'. See J. R. Green in Stainer 1901, pp. 34ff.; Midgley 1996, pp. 27ff.; and Darwall-Smith 2008, p. 315.

[54] See also note 32 to the poem on p. 83.

OWNERSHIP OF THE MS.

MS. Top. Oxon. d 287 is certainly the original manuscript with frequently untidy handwriting and with corrections added, not incorporated. It is not copied with care from an earlier draft.[55] Whether Elizabeth Sheppard found time to make a fair copy for Scrippy is unknown: if she did not then she may have passed this rough copy to her. In any case no pedigree of any kind tells us how it eventually came into the hands of Neville Egerton Leigh. He was a collector but he does not appear to have valued the MS. very highly. There is the possibility that Scrippy was an ancestor of his, but we do not know her married name and therefore cannot tell at present. For us the history of the document begins with the four modern letters now bound with it.[56]

THE FIRST TRANSCRIPT

In his 1930 letter to Bodley's Librarian, Arthur Cowley, donating the MS., Magrath, now 91 years old, says that he had had it transcribed for the printer just before the First World War but could no longer recall the name of the man he commissioned to do so (Appendix A, Letter 4). Another hand has added: 'This was P. Manning 24.vij. 30', and 'The transcript was in the hands of Warland Andrew of Bridge S^t. Abingdon in 1930, 3.xj.1930'. Percy Manning (1870–1917) was a local historian and folklorist who overcame disability to become a significant contributor to, and organiser of, antiquarian and folklore activity in Oxford.[57] In one of the scrapbooks he bequeathed to the Bodleian there is a letter to him from the Revd. H. E. Salter who asks in passing

---

[55] As well as the general untidiness of much of the MS. and the unclosed spaces left by overgenerous allowance for college summaries, note also the correction (below, pp. 55–6): 'I told you one thing wrong etc.'

[56] See text and notes in Appendix A.

[57] See obituary in Salter 1923, pp. 85ff., the *ODNB* entry, and Heaney 2017, chapter 1.

'How is Shepelinda [sic] progressing?'[58] Frank Warland Andrew, who somehow obtained Manning's transcript, was born in Sherborne, Dorset, in 1872.[59] He set up as a photographer with a studio in Abingdon. In 1930 he offered the transcript to John Lane (The Bodley Head) for publication, but it was refused because 'there are not enough of them [i.e. Memoirs] to make a book though a magazine article could, I think, quite well be got from them'.[60] The same year he sold the transcript to John Fulton, one of the founders of the Yale University Medical Historical Library, where it now resides.[61]

MODERN REFERENCES TO THE MS.

The Memoirs have been rarely used since Magrath. Margaret Crum included the poem incipits in her *First-line index of English poetry, 1500–1800 in manuscripts of the Bodleian Library* (1969), while the brief May Day reference in the Magdalen section (p. 55) is quoted by Roy Judge in an article on

[58]   MS. Top. Oxon. d 191 (fol. 261), letter dated 3 Aug. but without year. The letter continues: 'One hardly knows whether a volume will be needed next year or whether the Germans will have walked off with all our funds'. This refers to the *Collectanea* series of the Oxford Historical Society in which Magrath intended the MS. to be published (see note 6 above), and the war did indeed prevent any further volumes being published. It suggests that the year is 1914. I am grateful to Michael Heaney for drawing my attention to this letter.

[59]   http://www.rootschat.com/forum/index.php?topic=437001.0 (accessed 24 Jan. 2014).

[60]   Letter from B. H. Willets dated 28 Oct. 1930 preserved with the transcript. See next note.

[61]   I am grateful to Dr. Melissa Grafe, John R. Bumstead Librarian for Medical History, Cushing/Whitney Medical Library, Yale University, for this information and for supplying a scanned copy of the MS. The call number is *Manuscript 18th cent* +. The handwriting is small and neat, which proves that the transcript was not made by Percy Manning himself. Michael Heaney advises me that Manning's handwriting was very untidy and often difficult to make out. It may be that John Fulton either recopied the MS. or made a fair copy from a transcript by Manning which no longer survives. The first leaf of the Yale transcript is inscribed: 'John R Magrath, Queen's College, Oxford, 1904' in a hand not dissimilar to the transcription pages which follow.

'May Morning and Magdalen College, Oxford',[62] and the Hornblowing on May Day (below, p. 64) by Christine Bloxham and by Chris Koenig.[63] Christine Bloxham also quotes the accounts of Balliol Revels and the St. John's College Barber's song.[64] The present writer contributed the transcribed text of the New College section of the MS. to *New College Notes* [2012].[65]

---

[62] *Folklore*, vol. 97, no.1 (1986), p. 17 with n. 29.

[63] Bloxham 2002, pp. 63–4; 'May Day frolics in city and county', *Oxford Times*, 29 Apr. 2009: reprinted in Koenig 2013, p. 234.

[64] Bloxham 2005, pp. 173 and 179 respectively.

[65] W. Poole & G. Neate, 'Shepilinda on New College in 1738', in *New College Notes* [2012], http://www.new.ox.ac.uk/library-ncnotes by Dr. William Poole, Fellow Librarian and Archivist.

EDITORIAL NOTE

The present publication is complete and presents an unaltered text with no added punctuation. Lineation of the running prose section is not noted but is preserved in the poems. The notes have been compiled with the help of the archivists of the colleges who were each sent the relevant section of the Memoirs and asked to comment. Their elucidations are attributed by initials to which the key is given below. All the replies were helpful and several were enthusiastic at the revelation of so unexpected a source, and one occasionally enlivened by gossiping insight.

INITIALS OF COLLEGE ARCHIVISTS
CONTRIBUTING FOOTNOTES

AI	Amanda Ingram	*Pembroke*
AM	Andrew Mussell	*Lincoln*
AS	Anna Sander	*Balliol*
CD	Clifford Davies	*Wadham*
CJ	Christopher Jeens	*Jesus*
EB	Elizabeth Boardman	*Brasenose*
EG	Emma Goodrum	*Worcester*
JC	Judith Curthoys	*Christ Church*
JR	Julian Reid	*Corpus, Merton*
MR	Michael Riordan	*Queen's, St. John's*
PS	Paul Seaward	*Oriel*
RD-S	Robin Darwall-Smith	*Magdalen, University*
RP	Robert Petre	*Oriel*
WP	William Poole	*New*

TRANSCRIPTION CONVENTIONS

	beginning of new folio (when not at the beginning of a line as printed)
[ ]	[erased or destroyed text]
	[Also for editorial insertions]
italic	partially erased or destroyed text
< >	<accidentally omitted text restored by the editor>
{ }	{repeated or otherwise superfluous text}
~~Ag~~	letters crossed out in the manuscript
?	follows doubtful character
?abc?	doubtful word

THE MEMOIRS

Shepilinda's memoirs
of the City and
University
of
Oxford
Jan^{ry} 7th
1737/8
For Dear Scrippy

[WORCESTER]

Worcester College, formerly Gloucester Hall but con- *fol. 10r* verted into a College by Sr Thomas Cook[1] who gave a sum of money for a provost & 6 Fellows & some Schollars (but how many I am a Stranger to),[2] the present Provost is the Revnd Mr Wm Gower,[3] who is a Batchelour, the most amiable, & best deserving of any in Town; this College has nothing remarkable in it, except the Laboratory where Black Bess (my Namesake)[4] was Boiled, & made into Soop:[5]

---

[1] Sir Thomas Cookes, 2nd Baronet (1648–1701), twice married but childless, who left £10,000 to fund either a new or an existing college at Oxford where he had matriculated from Pembroke College in 1667. The charter and statutes for Worcester College received royal approval in 1714.

[2] The number does not appear to have been specified: 'With a number of Scholars' (Devereux & Griffiths 1976, p. 16). When the obstacles to releasing the Cookes money were overcome it was estimated that rebuilding would provide 'good conveniences for 60 scholars' (Daniel & Barker 1900, p. 177) but this may have been an exaggeration.

[3] William Gower, Provost from 1736 until he died in 1777 leaving extensive bequests to the College. [EG] Foster, *Alumni*: Gower, William, s. Thomas, of St. Nicholas, Worcester, gent. Worcester Coll., matric. 9 July 1715, aged 13; B.A. 1719, M.A. 18 Jan., 1721–2, B. & D.D. 1739, provost 1736, until his death 20 July 1777.

[4] The first occurrence of the familiar form of 'Shepilinda's' actual forename Elizabeth (which does not appear at all). The others are p. 30 'for Bess wont sputter out all she knows'; p. 55 'excuse our Bess'; and p. 73 'Miss Betty what are you in love'.

[5] See Appendix B.

here dwells the best Tutor in town, Viz: Mr Tottee,[6] &
at this time, it is graced by the English Consuls Son, one
Mr Black,[7] who was born at Cadiz in Spain.—the Library
is a fine room & handsomely built; & is now furnish'd
with Books by the Donation of George Clark Esqr, D^r
of the Civil Law, & member for the University who has
given besides the Books, and Manuscripts, a large sume of
Money, for the support of 6 Fellows & three Scholars,[8] & to
build hansome Rooms for them to Inhabit in;[9] the Provost
has one Garden, & the Fellows another; in the Midle of the
great Quadrangle (which is most Beautifully laid out, in
fine gravel Walks,) Stands a fine Rustick Tempietto[10] which
is looked upon, as a very great piece of Antiquity. Messieurs
Black & Amphlet[11] wrote verses upon the Queen's death[12]

6   John Tottie, a fellow of the College in 1738. Foster, *Alumni*: Tottie,
John, s. Daniel, of Eccleshall, co. Stafford, cler. Worcester Coll., matric 8 July
1721, aged 16; B.A. from Queen's Coll. 1725, M.A. from Worcester Coll. 1 Mar.
1727–8, canon Christ Church 1760, B. & D.D. 1760, archdeacon of Worcester
1742, rector of St. Martin's, Worcester, 1751 until his death 21 Nov. 1774. [EG/
GN]
7   George Charles Black, son of Charles Black of Cadiz, matric. 24 Mar.
1737 aged 14. B.A. 1740 [EG]. Charles was reassigned from Cadiz to Algiers in
1730 but was outmanoeuvred by the Swedish Consul, made unpopular with the
Bey, and was finally dismissed for incompetence in 1739. See Playfair 1884, pp.
177–83.
8   These were in addition to those already funded by the Cookes bequest.
9   George Clarke (1661–1736) reappears on p. 24, where it is explained that
Worcester benefited from his exasperation over the obstacles put up by the other
All Souls fellows to his making further benefactions to their college. See Tim
Clayton, 'Clarke: father and son', in Green & Horden 2007, pp. 117–31.
10   The College archives contain very little information about its buildings
in the eighteenth century. [EG] For a possible identification of the *tempietto* with
a feature in Loggan, see Bate & Goodman 2014, p. 101, and for the gardens in
general, ibid. pp. 100–3.
11   Joseph Amphlett, matric. 12 July 1735, aged 20. Additional details from
Foster, *Alumni*: s. of Joseph, of Clent, co. Stafford, arm. B.A. 1739, M.A. 26 Jan.,
1741–2, D.C.L. 1750, vicar of Bampton, Oxon., preb. of Carlisle, 1778. [EG]
12   Caroline of Brandenburg-Ansbach (Wilhelmina Charlotte Caroline,
born 1683) became the queen consort of King George II when he succeeded
to the throne in 1727, having married him in 1705. She was popular with the
country and was greatly mourned when she died on 20 Nov. 1737, less than two
months before the date of composition of the *Memoirs*. Her death is referred to

the pretiest posies you ever saw——[13]

[ST. JOHN'S]

I shall next turn my Eye to S[t] John's,[14] the President is D[r] Holmes,[15] (some time ago Vice Can:) a very well bred Man, (for he is vastly Civil[16] to the Ladies), & a <u>Batchelour</u>. This Coll. was formerly S[t] Bernards,[17] but they having (by some means or other) procured a very pretty, neat, Thigh Bone, of S[t] Johns,[18] turn'd off poor S[t] Bernard, {and} & Made S[t] John their Patron.——The College is regularly built there is two Quadrangles, in the outward one is the Chapell which is hansome, & the prettyest in Oxford, for the Ladies, who immediately upon their entrance, take

fol. 10v

again on p. 41 (her statue at Queen's) and p. 82 (the conceit that the Muses were swamped with requests for elegiac inspiration).

[13]   Worcester is the only college which does not have an added summary note of founder, number of Fellows, length of frontage, etc.

[14]   See also Shepilinda's poem 'Now you shall hear how the S[t] Johns men love Miss G-n-r' on p. 71.

[15]   William Holmes was President 1728–48. He did marry but it was not until March 1743 and then it was to a rich widow, Mrs Sarah England. He was a benefactor to the college on his death in 1748, as was his wife, when she died two years later. Out of the funds they left to it the College put up the Holmes Building, which stands to the south of Canterbury Quad. [MR] See Adams 1996, pp. 47ff.

[16]   Interestingly Hearne used the same word when describing a visit to Holmes: 'This [a new edition of Leland], it seems, is in opposition to me. He was wonderfully civil, & said such an edition would do my edition no hurt' (22 Dec. 1734) *Hearne*, vol. II (OHS lxxii), 405.

[17]   Shepilinda is deliberately straining the facts to highlight the humour of the thigh-bone story which follows. There was no continuity of institution at the dissolution of the monasteries, only the re-use of certain buildings. [MR/GN]

[18]   'We then went into the inner room [of St. John's College Library] which is famous for the *manuscripts, archives,* and curious *trinkets,* which it contains; the most remarkable of which are as follows; *St.* John *the* Baptist'*s thigh-bone …*' *Terrae-Filius,* no. 34 (11 May 1721). See Amhurst 1726, p. 187; Rivers 2004, pp. 266ff. with n. 19 ('Angela Williams, Assistant Librarian of St. John's College, told me in 1996 that in all likelihood the curious items Amhurst lists in this essay were indeed in the library'). Note that there is no thigh bone now!

place as Gentleman Commoners, or Masters of arts;[19] in
the Inward Quadrangle, over each Gate, is a fine Brass
Statue, one of K: C the 1st, & the other, of his Q:—the
Library is a large Hansome Room, & a great Number of
Books; by one of the Windows, hangs a very fine Picture,
of K: C: the 1st: drawn with a Pen & Ink, with the whole
Book of the readings[20] Psalms, wrote in his hair, legible to
fine good Eyes,[21]—in the Room beyond the Library are 2
Curious Skeletons,[22] the first ever put together with Wires,

[19] Obscure. There may be an implication that middle-ranking members of
colleges had a traditionally defined area of seating in the chapels, apparently
near the entrance, which, in St. John's, unaccompanied women shared.

[20] The OED entry 'reading psalms' quotes P. A. Scholes, The Great Dr.
Burney (London, 1948), I. vi. 59) as follows: 'There was, of course, in the churches
a clear distinction between the "reading psalms" (the prose psalms taken regularly,
in course according to the Prayer Book and read in alternate verses) and the
"singing psalms"'. Rivers 2004 says 'the drawing is much faded' and 'the Psalms
Amhurst mentions are not legible' (reporting the 1996 conversation).

[21] Baskerville has this description: 'Here is in the Library of this house the
Efigies of King Charles y[e] 1st drawne by a penman as far as the bust, containing
in the haires of his head, face, beard, other clothing, the whole booke of Psalmes,
Bishop Laud paid the Penman for this Curiosity' (Baskerville 1905, p. 193). Celia
Fiennes mistakenly describes the text as 'the whole Comon prayer' (Fiennes
1947, p. 35). Nicholas Amhurst also mentions it in the same list of 'trinkets'
as the thigh-bone (note 18 above) and adds the story of Charles II's visit when
he tried to persuade the college to give it to him. Also mentioned in Pocket
Companion 1756: 'Here likewise are some valuable curiosities, particularly the
famous Picture of King Charles I. which has the whole Book of Psalms written
in the Lines of the Face and the Hair of the Head' (p. 81). The drawing is still
in the Library and was examined in 2009 in the Oxford Colleges Consortium
for Conservation laboratory, and 'no clear script can be seen under normal
magnification'. See (with illustration) Cristina Neagu, 'Reading between the
lines: a micrographic portrait of King Charles I', Christ Church Library Newsletter,
vol. 5, issue 3 (Trinity 2009), pp. 20–2 with a final footnote adding that 'the script
has indeed been recently identified', but this has turned out to be mistaken.

[22] John Speed (1595–1640) the anatomist, son of the cartographer, 'was
the first anatomy lecturer in Oxford, and wrote a treatise which relates to two
skeletons which he made and gave to his college library' (ODNB). The treatise
includes very accomplished anatomical drawings: those of the two skeletons
show that they were mounted on wooden plinths and could be swung out of the
cupboards in which they were kept at each side of a partitioned off room at the
far end of the Laudian Library. [I am grateful to the Librarian Dr. Stewart Tiley
for showing me the volume and for his valuable explanation. GN]. The skeletons
were eventually transferred to the Museum of the History of Science. [MR]

| of a Man & a Woman—the Choir was given by Sr Will: *fol. 11r*
Petty; (or some such Body, I allmost forget tho.)[23] Mr Derham[24] Tutor in the College; (a charming Man) has a study;
most elegantly furnished not only with the most valuable
Books; but a very great Colection of rarities of all kinds,
one of which is not <to> be equald even in the Museum
it self; it is a wigg of a Sable Hue equal in Size, to four of
the largest Wiggs, that was ever Made;—it was formerly
the Property {of} of one Dr. Bridge lately Decease'd;[25] &
since Purchas'd not without a Great sum) by the present
possessour—The late owner, endow'd it with this great and
Wonderful, quality, that who ever wore it when Studying
Physick ; should learn more in one half Hour than all that
is Contain'd in both those Celebrated Authors Hippocrates
& Galen[26] besides this Wonderfull wonder of wonders is
one allmost as great Viz: a <u>Pretty Lord</u>[27]—the Founder S^r
Thomas White, who {who} before he died saw every one
of his College Protestants[28] (& yet was not angry) wrote a

[23] The choir had been closed soon after the foundation as the college
could not afford it but it was re-established by a gift from Sir William Paddy
(1554–1634), who had been a commoner of the college and was then doctor to
James I. [MR] See Adams 1996, pp. 32ff.

[24] William Derham was to succeed Holmes as President from 1748 to
1757 and was Whyte's Professor of Moral Philosophy. [MR] Foster, *Alumni*:
Derham, William, s. of William, of Upminster, Essex, cler. St. John's Coll.,
matric. 27 June 1721, aged 18; B.A. 1725, M.A. 1729, Proctor 1736, B.D.1737,
D.D. 1742, President 1748 until his death, 16 July 1757. He also appears a little
further on as the owner of a fine cat, and in the poem as Mr. D-r-m.

[25] The likeliest candidate, since 'lately deceased' is Foster, *Alumni*: Bridge,
William, s. Daniel, of London, pleb. St. John's Coll., matric. 1 July 1691, aged
18; fellow 1693–1737, B.A. 1695, M.A. 1699, B.Med. 1702, B.D. 1706, D.D. 1711,
born in Feb. 1674, entered Merchant Taylors' school 1684, vicar of Fyfield,
Oxon., rector of Cheam, Surrey, 1723, born in Fenchurch Street, 14 Feb. 1672–3
(Rawlinson), died 5 Sept 1737, buried in the chapel of his college.

[26] The miraculous wig appears to be undocumented elsewhere. [MR]

[27] Clearly a punning allusion but no St. John's Pretty/Pritty/Priddy etc.
has been identified.

[28] The college was founded under Mary and was undoubtedly part
of the re-Catholicisation of England. This, I think, explains the reference
to Protestants, but many of these official Protestants would, like Edmund
Campion, convert to Rome in the decade after the founder's death. [MR]

letter[29] to them about 10 Days before he died wherein he desired them to live in Brotherly love & Charity one with another This letter he desired might be legibly transcrib'd & Safely kept by every fellow in the College which request *fol. 11v* they have all Comply'd with & Some | {& some} of them, are wrote by the Ingenious, & Rev[n][d] Mr Parry;[30] the finest pen man (for ought I know) of any in Europe ; the Original Safely kept in the Archives,—I have one thing more to remark in this College, & that is, one day in the year, the College Barber, Sings a Song, to the Members, Call'd Adam Beck, & Shudledum, & hudledum agai[n] the drums beat thick & thick, but my Informer c[d] neither tell me the day that it is perform'd, nor the reason of this ancient Custom[31]—nay they are so very fond of vocal musick in this College that on{e} Xmas Day, & Xmas Eve, at 8 a clock at night, all the Gentlemen assemble together in the Hall & sing the Psalms for the day—There are many Cats in this College but Mr Derhams excelleth them all——

[29] The letter he wrote encouraging the fellows to be nice to each other is still given to each new fellow. Recently a mouse-mat version was produced. [MR] Hearne notes that Dr. Holmes (see above, note 15) 'hath just printed at the Theater, in a black Letter, upon one side of a broad sheet of paper, the last letter of Sir Thomas White, their founder, to the said College': (9 Feb. 1733/4) *Hearne*, vol. 11 (OHS lxxii), 302–3. Adams 1996 says that Holmes 'instituted a practice which is followed today. Copies of the Founder's last letter ... which he reproduced, are still ceremoniously presented to newly elected Fellows and scholars.' Before this one assumes they had to copy it out themselves (as the letter itself implies) or possibly ask for a new Parry copy (see next note). For the text, see Appendix C.

[30] William Parry (1687–1756) calligrapher, antiquary and numismatist, matric. from Jesus College, Oxford, on 19 Feb. 1705–6, and was eventually elected to a fellowship in his college. 'Parry's elegant hand, resembling the italic print, was much admired. Contemporaries considered some of his manuscripts to be so neatly written that they might be mistaken for well-executed typography. Several manuscripts transcribed by him are extant in the Bodleian Library, and a beautiful transcript which he made of the statutes of his college is preserved among its archives' (*ODNB*). Cf. *Pocket Companion 1756*, p. 70.

[31] The passage about the barber, including the song, is not known from other sources. [MR/GN]

This College was founded by Sr Tho: White in the year
1555 it has a president & 50 Fellows & Schollars an Organist
& singing Men & Chorister[s] The Bishop of Winchester
is Visitor its length is 217 feet——

[BALLIOL]

Now little Scrippy, I'll put my pattens on, & trudge it to   *fol. 12r '5'*
Belial,[32] (I beg pardon, I mean Baliol,) & there is a Master,[33]
a little tiny Man With a Huge Bagg full of Sense, in his
head, & many packets of good Humours in his pockets
which he liberaly bestows upon every occasion, he is a
Great Punster & a very good Disciplinarian—(poor Man)
he is Married—& has a Wife & one Child a Daughter[34]
who has a large share of her Father Dr. Leighs Wit, and
will after his Death—be in possession of it all; (an ample
Competency.) There is no likelyhood of the Familys being
encreas'd at present.[35]—There are many parcells of Building
in this College (Couzen Hoby's[36] are the best) tho none of
them are quite elegant, the part that the fellows Inhabit
was formerly an Inn (the Sign I forget as much as if I had

[32]   The same pun was made (but more ponderously) by *Terrae-Filius* in 1733:
'The worthy Head and Men of Balliol (I mean Belial, for I believe it should be
so spelt, since they are wicked enough to deserve that Title)' (Amhurst 1733,
pp. 5ff.).
[33]   Theophilus Leigh, Master 1726–83 (Vice-Chancellor 1738–41). 'Received
opinion would have us believe that the election of Theophilus Leigh was
scandalous, corrupt, and nepotistic': thus John Jones, introducing his account
of the contest (Jones 1997, pp. 155–60).
[34]   Cassandra, who would marry Samuel Cooke, elected Fellow of Balliol
in 1762, and would name their sons Theophilus Leigh Cooke and George Leigh
Cooke.
[35]   In fact there was to be a second daughter, Mary. She would marry her
cousin Thomas Leigh: see the table in Jones 1997, p. 116.
[36]   Foster, *Alumni*: Hoby, (Sir) Philip (Bart.), s. Thomas, of Somerly, Hants.
baronet. Balliol coll., matric. 7 Nov. 1732, aged 16; B.A. 1736, M.A. 1739, created
D.C.L. 14 Apr. 1749, of Marlow, Bucks., 5th baronet, chancellor of St. Patrick's,
Dublin, and dean of Ardfert 1748 until his death 29 June 1766. See also Dallaway
1815, p. 233 (chart).

fol. 12v '6'   never heard of it)[37]—| The Masters Lodgings are Bad, (& Inconvenient) only one fine large Room (which by the way my Mamma often longs for.) As for the outlet[38] it is but small ; the most copious of which, is a place commonly call'd (at least by all the Members of the Coll;) the Grove, but by others The Masters Wood Yard, or *[2 words erased]* Court, & there are two small Gardens, the Masters & the fellows, they are neither pretty, nor ugly, but what we call SoSo,—the Chapell is neat,[39] the painting in the Windows[40] Midlingly Well;—especially that, wherein Phillip is Baptizing the Eunuch, & King Hezekiah{,} is Sorely Sick,[41]— the Ante-Chapell, (where I pray when there—) is very Cold, they have one night in the year, that is Call'd Baliol Revells, it is in Winter, but I cannot say the Month,—This Night, all the Young Gay—Striplings of the College ; are their own Masters as no one can Controul them, their Custom is to Stand at the gate, & pick up, who ever they Meet ; (without regard either to Sex,[42] quality, or age,) & carry them into the Coll: Hall: & then, Setting them astride upon a Brass Eagle,[43] that is in the Midle of it: make

[37] The southern part of the west side included the site of the Catherine Wheel inn (leased from the college), which became the site of the Bristol Building erected in about 1720. The Fisher Building in the corner was not added until 1759. See Jones 1997, plans II–III on pp. 338ff.

[38] 'outlet' seems to have here the sense which *OED* describes as regional to Cheshire: 'A field, yard, or other enclosure attached to a house' (outlet, note 4b). Cf. *Pocket Companion 1756*, p. 32. 'One unparalleled Beauty belonging to this College [Magdalen] is the extensive Out-let' (going on to describe the Grove, the Walks, etc.).

[39] The chapel Shepilinda saw was demolished in 1856 and a new chapel built: *VCH Oxon*. iii. 91.

[40] By Abraham van Linge. 'They were the gifts of Richard Atkyns and Peter Wentworth in 1637. Both of these windows survive, although both are now divided into two': ibid.

[41] Black and white photograph in Davis 1963, third plate following p. 292. The caption gives the date as 1637.

[42] Written over erased 'Dress'.

[43] The great brass eagle lectern in the Chapel dates from about 1630 and was the gift of Edward Wilson. See Jones 1997 (colour plates C.15, C.16). Shepilinda and Hearne (see next note) both place it in the Hall. Unless there were two eagle

them tell a Story & after that, they generally make them very Drunk.—this sport lasts no longer than till 9 a clock. at which time the Master, & tutors, resume their Wonted power.—| last Revell was two years <ago> they were very near as (I was informed) demolishing an Old Woman, but this I can't positively affirm the Author being (tho' a man of great veracity) a vast Joker.[44] *fol. 13r '7'*

Balliol College was begun to be Erected by John Balliol Father to the King of Scots, & Dargavilla, or (Devoragilla ^{his wife}. He began it in the year 1262 and She, after his death, completed it, it consists, of a large Quadrangle on the North Side of which is the Chappell and the library furnisht with a Noble Collection of Books. The Visitor is Chosen by the College, which has a Master 12 fellows. &c, its length is 190 feet 6 Inches——

[TRINITY]

Trinity College will not long employ my pen, i[t] has a president, one Dr Hutsford,[45] a <u>Married Man</u>, he has one *fol. 13v '8'*

lecterns it must have been carried from Chapel to Hall for each Balliol Revels celebration, a far from trivial journey considering the distance and the steep incline of the Hall stairs.

[44] He was indeed a joker. Hearne gives the facts, tame by comparison with this lurid account: 'There is a Custom at Balliol College, for every Freshman on the Ist of Nov., when they begin to keep Fires, each of them to tell in his turn a story, the Seniors being Auditors, & the Dean of the College is present to see Things regular. It is done in the Hall at the Eagle, & there is afterwards a Collation, every junior contributing something. No Gown is excepted.' : (6 Nov. 1727) *Hearne*, vol. 9 (OHS lxv), 367). For the similar initiation rituals (but accompanied by 'salting' and 'tucking' penalties) at Merton and Pembroke in the previous century, see Johnson 1928, pp. 222ff.

[45] George Huddesford, President 1731–76: '[His] Presidency lasted for forty-four years and 292 days, a college record that seems unlikely ever to be broken. His years of office were pleasantly lacking in dramatic events, notable mainly for the development of antiquarian interest in the College's past' (Hopkins 2005, p. 166).

son only[46].—a proper Match for a Bal[liol] Daughter.[47]
There are many Fellows in this College The Chappell here[48]
is very neat, & very Sweet, it being Wainscoted with wood
of Lebanus,—& finely fineer'd—in the Cieling their is the
whole Passion of our Saviour[49] finely express'd in Stucc[o]
work & the whole is most Elegantly done.[50]—the Garden
is allways engageingly ?retired?, and Beautifully laid out in
Walks ; there is a Smal[l] Laborinth, & a pretty Fountain
which adds much to its Variety.—nothing else here claims
a Share of my Observation.——

fol. 14r '9' Trinity College, formerly Durham College, founded in
1350 by Thomas Hatfield B[p] of that See, for the benefit of
the Monks of Durham but disolv'd at the Reformation &
purchas'd by S[r] Thomas Pope, who endow'd & repair'd it
& named it trinity College, it Consists of 2 Quadrangles,

[46] His (first) wife was Elizabeth 'whose family origins are uncertain'
(*ODNB*). William, the first of three sons, was to become a conscientious Keeper
of the Ashmolean and biographer of antiquarians. He was six years old at the
time of Shepilinda's Memoir. Foster, *Alumni*: Huddesford, William, s. George,
of Oxford, doctor. Trinity Coll., matric. 20 Oct. 1749, aged 17; B.A. 1753, MA.
1756, B.D. 1767, Proctor 1765, keeper of the Ashmolean Museum 1755–72.

[47] Referring to Cassandra Leigh (p. 9 above), but Shepilinda's suggested
marriage did not happen.

[48] See now Kemp 2013.

[49] The work of the Huguenot refugee Pierre Berchet (Hopkins 2005,
p. 157). Celia Fiennes (see next note) is right and Shepilinda is mistaken: the
painting is of the Ascension rather than the 'whole Passion'.

[50] Noted by Celia Fiennes in *c.* 1695: 'Trinity Colledge Chapple which was
not finish'd the last tyme I was at Oxford, but now is a beautifull magnificent
Structure, its lofty and curiously painted the rooffe and sides the history of
Christ's ascension and very fine Carving of thin white wood just like that
at Windsor, it being the same hand, the whole Chappel is wanscoated with
Walnut-tree and the fine sweet wood the same which the Lord Orfford brought
over when High Admiral of England and has wanscoated his hall and staircase
with, it is sweet like Cedar and of a reddish coullour, but the graine much finer
and well vein'd' (Fiennes 1947, pp. 36ff.). Also by von Uffenbach in 1710: 'the
chapel of this college is incomparably beautiful and is built in the Italian style
without a ceiling, Inside it is decorated all over with genuine cedarwood, so that
when one enters the chapel it not only presents an incomparable appearance,
but also gives off a thoroughly agreeable and excellent perfume' (von Uffenbach
1928, p. 24). See also Hopkins 2005, pp. 153–62.

in the 1ˢᵗ are the Chapell and the Hall & the library.—The Chappell is Wonderfully Elegant; the Garden is large & delightfull,—this Society has a president 12 fellows, 12 scholars &c—the Bᵖ of Winchester is the Visitor,——

[EXETER]

I will now take a Trip into the Turl, & there I shall find the College of Exeter, but now I have found it, what shall I see there? No Antiques ; there is Indeed a Rector, one Mr Edgecomb,[51] a Batchelour in Divinity ; & a <u>Batchelour Indeed</u> ; some Graduates, & under Graduates of all Sorts,— the Late Rector was one Dʳ Atwell,[52] (I believe a Civilian, I am sure not a divine),[53] but he being a lover of Learning, resign'd his headship, to pursue his studies ; he is at present, engaged in a paper War,[54] With one Mʳ Marshal,[55] Rector of

fol. 14v '10'

[51] James Edgcumbe (1705–50) from Tavistock, matr. 1722, fellow 1728, Rector 1737–50.

[52] Foster, *Alumni*: Atwell, Joseph, s. M[athew], of Buckland Monachorum, Devon, cler. Exeter Coll., matr. 12 Apr. 1712, aged 16; B.A. 1715, fellow 1718, M.A. 1718, B.D. 1728, rector 1733–7, D.D. 1738, took priests orders 1736, preb. of Southwell 1737, of Gloucester 1737, and of York 1739, rector of Oddington, co. Gloucester, 1739, vicar of Fairford 1738, canon of Westminster 1759, died before 11 Aug. 1768. See Boase 1894, p. 90. Boase also notes (p. 314, n. 1) that 'the windows of the Dining Room … were glazed in 1733 by Dʳ Atwell in the manner of Italian Balcony-windows, which let in Pools of Water in rainy Weather' and had to be reglazed in 1785. As Rector, Atwell attempted to deal with non-residency and other problems of the college but met with limited success. (*VCH Oxon*. iii. 111).

[53] He was ordained two years earlier but did not become Doctor of Divinity until the year of the *Memoirs*. (See preceding note.)

[54] The original controversy was between William Whiston and Arthur Ashley Sykes and was whether the date given in the fragment of Phlegon of Tralles reporting darkness in the daytime allowed identification with that accompanying the Crucifixion. I cannot find that the 'paper war' between Atwell and Marshall actually reached print but Shepilinda's description suggests that their controversy may rather have concerned the awkward possibility that if the darkness was a natural event of the kind which could be calculated in advance by a Kepler or a Newton then it was not a miraculous manifestation of horror at the sinfulness of the Crucifixion.

[55] Foster, *Alumni*: Marshall, Benjamin, s. Ben. of London (city), gent. Christ Church, matric. 23 Mar. 1699/1700, aged 17; student 1701, B.A. 1703,

Nanton,[56] (& one of the Bp of Gloucester's Rural Deans). The subject is upon the Remaining Scraps of Phlegon, whether the Eclips[e] at our Saviour's Death was natural, [or] Not.[57]—& when it is finish'd of what use will it be— Exeter's, done with now:——

fol. 15r '11' Exeter College was Founded by Walter Stapledon B^p of Exeter who in 1314 having Establish'd a Society in Hart & Arthur Halls, for the Conveniency of More room, he 2 years after, translated it to this place, the learned Narcissus Marsh late AB^p of Armagh contributed near 1400 p^{nds} towards the new Building this College, which has Made the Quadrangle neatly Regular & Beautifully Uniform—it has a Rector 23 Fellows &c—the Visitor is the B^p of Exeter its Length is 200 feet——

[JESUS]

fol. 15v '12' To Jesus[58] next I must turn my Wandring Eyes the College of Ancient Brittains, in this Coll every one is a Gentleman, by Birth; they have not many valuable curiositys for they are not very great lovers of Antiquity.—being all persons of too great passions, to be long pleased with any thing.—Sr Watkin Williams Wynne[59] was of this College,

M.A. 1706, rector of Naunton, co. Gloucester, 1711, canon of Lichfield 1728, rector of Allesley, co. Warwick, 1740.

56 i.e. Naunton, 'a parish in the hundred of Slaughter, Gloucester, 6 miles from Stow-in-the-Wold … containing 83 houses and 433 inhabitants. The church is a very handsome building. It is a rectory, value 16*l.* 13*s.* 4*d.* in the patronage of the bishop of Worcester' (Capper 1808, s.n.). Benjamin Marshall was Rector of St. Lawrence Church, Naunton, from 1711 to 1740. A modern notice inside the church listing the rectors notes that 'He completed the Register'.

57 Marshall 1725, pp. 195ff. (footnote) argues for the identification with the darkness accompanying the Crucifixion without mentioning Atwell.

58 The line ends of this fol. are preserved at the left edge of fol. 74r.

59 There is a good and substantial article on Sir Watkin Williams Wynn in *ODNB*, describing him as an archetypal Tory of the Hanoverian era and, in passing, noting that he was educated at Ruthin School and Jesus College, Oxford, 'where he had a record of idleness and extravagance'. This sits well with the punchbowl and ladle made by John White of London in 1726/7, which he

& when he left it, he (knowing that all the memmbers were lamentably aflicted with a Thirst,) gave a prodigious large Silver punch Bowl big enough allmost for the members to Swim in which is reckon'd the most curious piece of plate in Oxford ; the ladle which holds a good Winchester pint[60] is given full to every Stranger of Worship, that Comes into the college, to Drink Sr Watkins health which by all honest Jovial Tory Topers, is reciev'd With great Glee,—here is a principle one Dr Pardoe,[61] all as I know or can say of him

gave in 1732 and which the College still possesses. Six years later Shepilinda gives the first attestation of the large ladle capacity except that later versions have half a pint, not a full pint ('a full Winchester half pint' in *Companion* 1762, p. 26), which suggests that her memory played her false on this occasion. She does not mention the capacity of the bowl itself, which later accounts up to the present solemnly assert to be ten gallons (ibid.; *Guide* 1827, p. 104; Clifford 2004, p. 27b), although the bowl has a diameter of about 19 inches and a height of one foot, of which a third is pedestal. The ladle, too, looks to hold only about a quarter of a standard pint. [CJ/GN] In her 2004 work accompanying an Ashmolean exhibition of Oxford college silver Helen Clifford has this description: Sir William gave several gifts of silver to his old college] including an enormous silver-gilt punch bowl of 1726/7, weighing just over 278 oz, engraved with his name and date of his gift: 'D.D. Watkin Williams Wynn de Wynstay in Com. Denbigh. L.L.D: olim hujus Collegii Socio Commensalis 1732.' The Bursar recorded 9s 9d for wine in 1733 upon receiving Wynn's fine bowl, and presumably drunk from it. It is so large (it holds ten gallons) that baptisms for the new born of College members are sometime performed in it. By tradition, although there is no proof, Williams Wynn is supposed to have promised to provide an even larger bowl if anyone could claim to have filled it with punch and drunk it in one go, the current bowl being the prize. It appears that, as yet, no-one has been able to meet the challenge. It was probably this punch bowl that was used at a dinner in the Radcliffe Camera in June 1814 during the visit of the Prince Regent, the Emperor of Russia, and the King of Prussia to Oxford. Hakewill, a guest at the event, noted that 'There had been a large gold bowl from (blank) College, which holds (blank) gallons, set before Blucher, filled with punch' from which 'we all took a glass and drank to his health and the sovereigns' (Clifford 2004, pp. 27ff. with fig. 27, describing no. 79 in the exhibition).

60   i.e. a standard pint defined by the appropriate measuring vessel among those originally deposited at Winchester (so *OED* 'Winchester' n., 1a).

61   Thomas Pardo was from Kidwelly, Carmarthen. He matriculated in 1704, became a Fellow in 1711 and Principal in 1727, remaining so until his death in 1763. He was also Chancellor of St. David's 1749–53. Three of his account books survive and Baker 1971, p. 26 has an interesting exploration from evidence in these accounts of the possibility that Pardo befriended and promoted the

is,—he is a Justice of peace.—I believe there is a good many fellows of this Coll. Mr Apperly^62 one, if he is a Sample of the rest, I wish them a good night NB there is a fine Scrubbing Post^63 here^64 for the use of the Man[y] Member[s]^65

fol. 16r '13' Jesus College^66 claims Queen Elizabeth for its founder, but it was Actually^67 begun by Hugh Price Doctor of Law AD 1571 who had a Charter from that Glorious Queen for that purpose.—it now has a Principal 16 Fellows, 16 Scholars 8 Exhibitioners &c.—and Consists of two handsome Quadrangles, the innermost very regular & Uniform. The Earl of Pembroke is Visitor.—its length is 133 feet.——

college employment of a poor boy who went on to be the College Butler, James Matthews. There is a portrait of Pardo, hung in the Hall [CJ]. The portrait is described in Lane Poole 1926, vol. 2, p. 203 (no. XVI.27).

62 'Mr Apperly' might be James Apperley (Fellow 1725–37) but more likely his brother Anthony Apperley (Fellow 1735–40). They were from Herefordshire. Foster would appear to list both, giving their father as Thomas Apperley of Hereford, college as Jesus, and matriculation dates of 1725 and 1729 respectively. He does not however record that they became Fellows of the College. [CJ]

63 Use of a 'scrubbing post' is said to be characteristic of Scots and Welsh. 'An antient *Britton* might as easily have been charmed from his scrubbing Post' (James Drake, *The antient and modern stages surveyd* (London, 1699), p. 94). 'Besides these general subjects, there are others which, like the stage-tricks, will always ensure the suffrages of the vulgar; among them are national jokes, as … a Scotchman with his scrubbing-post' (Francis Grose et al., *The Antiquarian repertory* (London, 1807), vol. 1, p. 19). In a cartoon set of 1792 attacking Lord Bute entitled *The Posts* there is a drawing described by Edward Hawkins in these terms: 'The second design is *The Scrubbing Post*, and shows a very rough post, or trunk of a tree, by the side of a road and, like a term, having the head of a satyr carved out of its summit. Against the post a gaunt Scotchman is energetically scrubbing his back. Lord Bute looks with a benevolent smile at the pleasure of his countryman … Below are these lines: To Scrubb one self where'ere it itches / Is better far than Cloths and Riches'. (Stephens 1883, pp. 164–6, no. 3944). [CJ/GN]

64 There is no record of a wooden post, stone pillar or menhir which might be used, or referred to disparagingly, as a scrubbing-post.

65 'ber[s]' is written above 'Mem' to fit in the page width. 'Man*g*y' is a tempting (but not compelling) restoration of the damaged preceding word.

66 The second passage, referring to the College's foundation, is the standard account and correctly recognises the role of Hugh Price of Brecon. [CJ]

67 'it was Actually' is written over erased 'afterward'.

[LINCOLN]

I will next retire to Lincoln, but I want the skill of the most *fol. 16v '14'*
Eminent Poets to describe the many good things belongin[g]
to this Wonerfull College, the Worthy Rector is the Rev^{nd}
Dr Isham,[68]Younger Brother to Sr Edmund Isham Bar^t. an
Ancient Family; he is at present a <u>Batchelor</u> but not entirely
out of hopes of being Soon Married to the Eldest Daughter
of the Rev Dr Pantin[69] Master of Pembroke. NB her grandmother is dead).[70] The Chappell is neat and lighted by the
12 Apostles[71] so it does not want for Illuminations, they are
prettily Painted, (but Scrip says they are not so well Done
nor so elegantly express'd as the Vine Windows)[72] The rest
of the Chapell has an agreable neat plainness The Master's
Lodgings are Magnificent, as are all his Entertainments; his
Accomplishments are numerous, & his Manners the most
polite,—his person agreeable enough for one of his age,
which is 40 or thereabouts, rather more than less; NB his
nose is too little for the Breadth of his face[73] which is pink

[68] Euseby Isham was certainly one of the college's best-connected and
most presentable Rectors (1731–55). [AM] Foster, *Alumni*: Isham, Euseby, s.
Justinian, of Lamport, Northants., baronet. Balliol Coll., matric. 22 Oct. 1716,
aged 18, B.A. 1718; Lincoln Coll. M.A. 1721, B. & D.D. 1733, Rector 1731–55,
Vice-Chancellor 1744–7, rector of Lamport and Hazelbeach, died 17 June 1755.

[69] Rev. Matthew Panting, also referred to on p. 47 (Pembroke).

[70] He did marry Elizabeth Panting in 1739, but had previously turned down
at least one advantageous offer of marriage, so was scarcely 'out of hopes'; he
had once said that he thought a Head of House should resign on marriage, which
it turned out he did not, so perhaps he was re-thinking his position. [AM]

[71] The Van Linge Apostles in the Chapel windows are as they were, only
better, since restoration a few years ago. [AM]

[72] The stained glass windows in the private chapel of the Vyne, a Tudor
mansion in Sherborne St. John, near Basingstoke, are considered to be among
the most beautiful examples of sixteenth-century glass in Europe. The three
windows depict (right to left) Margaret Tudor, Henry VIII, and Catherine of
Aragon below, respectively, the Passion, Crucifixion and Resurrection. [In 2015
the windows were removed for conservation by the National Trust.]

[73] His 1737 portrait in the Hall, by Thomas Gibson, is described by Lane
Poole 1926, vol. 1, p. 177 (no. VIII.19). The illustration in Green 1979 (pl. facing
p. 340) shows, in this editor's view, that Shepilinda had a point but opinions will
no doubt vary.

fol. 17r '15' Coulour; his height the tallest of any pate in Oxford | He
has at this time one of the handsomest, & most Irregular &
Rakish, Gentlemen Commoner;[74] that ever ruled the Roast
in Oxford, his name is Robinson[75] & is of the Same County
with the Head,—in this College, (or at least without Side
of it) formerly the Devil took his Station,[76] upon one of
the top Pinnacles, but by the Wonderfull Grace & Worth
of the present Incumbent (& the help of a high Wind) his
Devilship is quite demolish'd—and never a one as yet in his
room,—which makes some people think, that he was in too
frigid an Element, & therefore chose, to come farther into
the College; for most of the Rooms there are warm & of
Consequence much more fit for his Torrid Constitution,—I
know no Customs they have in this College except Gaming & Guzzling honest Coll: ale which all the Members
do without Stint they (as it is the Custom) go to prayers
twice a Day——

fol. 17v '16' Lincoln College, is of the Foundation of Richard Fleming,
Bishop of Lincoln. it was begun in 1427 and design'd for

---

74 *Commoner* is written over *Comoners*. Shepilinda did not fully disentangle
her singular and plural versions: Robinson as the handsomest etc. or Robinson
as one of the handsomest etc.

75 Robinson the Gentleman Commoner was apparently John Robinson,
son of John Robinson of Cransley, Northants., matric. 1 Feb 1736/7, aged 17.
He went on to join the Middle Temple. [AM]

76 The Lincoln Devil, a grotesque carving of a crouching devil (not to be
confused with the *Lincoln imp*), was situated at the Western end of the North
gable but lost its head in a storm in 1731 and was taken down two years later.
'Rumour suggested he had migrated to Brasenose' (Green 1979, p. 722). A
new devil based on a Loggan drawing was carved in 2003. [GN] Probably the
most interesting thing here is the allusion to the phrase *The Devil over Lincoln*,
with which the writer seems very familiar. The earliest reference I'm aware
of to the expression relating to the college rather than to the cathedral is in
Ray's 'Proverbs' in 1737, and this runs it very close. [AM] 'To look on one as
the Devil looks over *Lincoln*.' Some refer this to *Lincoln* minster, over which
when first finished the Devil is supposed to have looked with a torve and
terrick countenance, as envying mens costly devotion, saith Dr *Fuller*; but more
probable it is that it took its rise from a small image of the Devil standing on
the top of *Lincoln* College in Oxford': Ray 1737, p. 224.

a Seminary of Divines with a View to confute Wickliffs Tenets.[77] Rotherham and the Bishop of the Sam[e] See Completed the Building in 1475 & Augmented its Revenues. it has a Rector 12 Fellows, 2 Chaplains. & the Bishop of Lincoln is Visitor. its length is 207 feet 6 inches——

[BRASENOSE]

The Brazen Nose next Demands my Attention & first I will tell you a Strange Story belongs to this Coll: of one Fryar Bacon[78] who studied so long till he made himself perfect in the art of Necromancy—this Scholar Made a Brazen head which one time or other was to Speak & if the Words it utter'd were heard (every one:) England was to be enclosed with a Brazen Wall & be impenetrable to all Foreign Forces, but the person that they set to watch it not being of the Carefull kind was dilatory even in so Important an affair—& when the Mighty head began to speak he was asleep & waked to hear no more then Time is, Time past, & Time to come[79]—which words if you can find the meaning of you will know more then I can tell you—but however in Memory of this the College still preserves a Brazen Nose without the College; & Brazen heads and Faces within the College;—of which Dr Ship-

fol. 18r '17'

---

[77] Fleming had lived in Queen's for some years just as Wycliffe had done. He had been accused of Wycliffite views by Archbishop Arundel and became a strenuous enemy of such views. See Green 1979, pp. 2ff.

[78] 'A ... legend ... associated the College with the scientist and scholar Roger Bacon, and further embroidery connected the "brass nose", with his magical prophetic head of brass as described, for instance, in Robert Greene's play *Friar Bacon and Friar Bungay* (1588). Very possibly the large nose which overhangs the gate of the College once graced the entrance to Brasenose Hall.' See Evans and Richards 1983, p. 3. [EB]

[79] The point in the Greene play and the earlier *Famous Historie of Fryer Bacon* is that the boy should have wakened the Friar after the first utterance so that aphorisms would have been heard and 'England had been circled round with brass.' The third utterance destroyed the head and with it Bacon's 'life, fame and glory'.

fol. 18v '18' pen[80,] is <u>Principle</u> ^{Principal} | a very fit Governor[81] for Such a Society—he now & then Borrows a Parliamentary Phraze or two from his B[r] the Worthy Will: Shippen.[82] I can say no more of him or his College than he is—a Man Without a Wife.[83]

[80] 'If sources are to be believed Robert Shippen (1675–1745) was sly, lecherous, corrupt, covetous, unscrupulous, selfish, immoral and could be relied upon to give support where he saw his own advantage' (Elizabeth Boardman, 'The Principals of Brasenose' in *The Brazen Nose*, vol. 36 (2002), 32, referring also to 'An Oxford Don Two Hundred Years Ago' an unpublished manuscript life of Robert Shippen by Reginald W. Jeffery: Brasenose College Archives MPP 56 F4/10). [EB] Foster, *Alumni*: Shippen, Robert, s. William, of Chester (city), doctoris. Merton Coll., matric. 6 Apr. 1693, aged 16, B.A. 1696; fellow Brasenose Coll., M.A. 1699, B. and D.D. 1710; Master of that college 1710–45, Vice-Chancellor 1718–23; baptised at Prestbury 27 July 1675, professor of music at Gresham College 1705–10. Presented rector of Great Billing, Northants. 1710, of Whitechapel, Middx. 1716, and of Amersham, Bucks. 1744; died 24 Nov. 1745, buried in the college chapel. See Rawl. vi. 78, and xxi. 102; Gutch, i. 375. See also *ODNB*.

[81] 'Much of our information about ... Robert Shippen, comes from the pen of Thomas Hearne (1678–1735), never noted for his balanced reporting. He records every possible scandal he can find about Shippen with considerable malice, describing him, for example, as "a most lecherous man" and "a strange lover of Women". He records that Shippen used "to go often to" the wife of the President of Trinity [George Huddesford] and that he "debauched a very pretty Woman, one M[rs]. Churchill, the wife and afterwards the widow of one Churchill, a bookbinder in Oxford, one of the prettiest Women in England. He poxed her, of which she died in a sad Condition. The thing is so notorious that 'tis frequently talked of to this day"': Elizabeth Boardman, 'Escaping suspicion: women in Brasenose before 1974', *The Brazen Nose*, vol. 33 (1999), 24, referring to Hearne (22 Feb. and 22 Mar.1731/2 in *Hearne*, vol. 11 (OHS lxxii), 31, 34). [EB] Robert is also mentioned on p. 58 below, as arranging the marriage of his nephew, Robert Leyborne.

[82] William Shippen (1673–1743) was a Jacobite and a Tory politician eventually representing Newton, Lancs., and performing well in the Jacobite interest in Parliament. Foster, *Alumni*: Shippen, William, s. William, of Prestbury, Cheshire, S.T.D. Brasenose Coll., matric. 16 July 1687, aged 14; baptised at Prestbury 30 July 1673, B.A. from Trinity Coll., Cambridge, 1694–5, from Westminster School; bar.-at-law Middle Temple, 1693, M.P. Bramber Dec. 1707–13, Saltash 1713–15, and Newton, Co. Lancaster, in 5 parliaments 1715, until his death 1 May 1743; buried in St. Andrew, Holborn. See also *ODNB*.

[83] 'He had married Frances, the widow of Sir Gilbert Clarke, as her fourth husband and brought her home to the College on 24 October 1710, within five months of his election as Principal ... Hearne ... reports her death on 29 September 1728': Elizabeth Boardman *loc. cit.* See (3 Oct. 1728) *Hearne*, vol. 10

Brazen Nose College takes its name from Brazen Nose Hall
which formerly stood on this spot.[84] It was founded AD
1509 by Wm Smith then B^p of Litchfield & Coventry but
afterwards of Lincoln & Wm Sutton Esqr: It has a Principal
20 Fellows 33 exhibitioners &c—It consists of 2 handsome Quadrangles in the lesser of which are the Chappel
& Library, & under them a wide and pleasant Cloyster very
compactly and elegantly Built. The Visitor is the Bishop of
Lincoln its length is 259 feet 6 inches

[ALL SOULS]

All Souls I shall next endeavour to set forth in its proper   *fol. 19r '19'*
Colours and I will paint it well as my poor weak Genius
will permit me—this College was founded by Arch=Bishop
Chichely a very Good Man—(God rest his soul) The Chappell
here is grave, Solemn & Awefully fine—it is all pannell'd with
Marble round the altar,[85]—in one piece of Marble is a very
Curious Rasher of Bacon[86] fit to put upon the Coals & is most

(OHS lxvii), 53 where he also notes that her maiden name was Leigh and that
'She was a very proud woman, given much to drinking and gaming, and did no
good.' She seems to have retained the title 'the Lady Clarke'.

[84] 'Brasenose College takes its name and part of its site from a medieval
Oxford hall, one of the many which, beginning as unofficial lodging-houses,
gradually evolved into more formal institutions of learning. There were several
such halls on the land now occupied by the College, and some time about 1270
the word "Brasenose" is found in documents relating to one of them. Little is
known about Brasenose Hall': Evans & Richards 1983. [EB]

[85] 'Clarke used his position at the Admiralty to get the marble for the All
Souls Chapel from Genoa' (Tim Clayton in Green & Horden 2007, p. 123). 'The
Altar-Piece is of beautiful clouded marble' (*Pocket Companion 1756*, p. 52). It was
eventually removed as part of the conversion of the Italianate style altar and
East wall into an acceptable Gothic Revival form in the 1870s, and was sold for
£113 (Sparrow 1960a, p. 6). An oil painting on canvas by 'Green' (precise identity
unknown) of the East end of the Chapel as Shepilinda would have seen it was
obtained by the college at auction in 1959 (Sparrow 1960, p. 452 with fig. 50)
and is illustrated (in black and white only) in Colvin & Simmons 1989, p. 50.
There is a good longer view in Ackermann 1814, vol. I, p. 218 (acquatint by F.
Mackenzie) showing the colour and extent of the marble but with Meng's *Noli
me tangere* substituted (in 1773) for the central panel behind the table.

[86] The 'Green' painting is inaccessible at the time of writing, but it is in

Daintily express'd in its proper Coulours—The painting of
the altar piece is the pious Founder being carried to heaven &
there reciev'd[87] it is very well painted but by what hand I know
not so I won't lye about the Matter, [in another hand] *Js Thornhill* the
Hall is a very handsome Room some good Pictures but I do
not know what any of them are except the Founders[88] which

fol. 19v '20' hangs at the upper end, over the high Table—| There is the
most neat Gray Marble Chimney=piece I ever saw—a very
good Grate & generally a pretty good Fire (at least there was
when Scrip & I were there) The Library is very handsome
but no books in it;[89] the Members generally Studying at the
three Tunns;[90] of which the Inimitable Widow Bradgate[91] is

any case unlikely that the artist was so meticulous that Shepilinda's rasher-like
swirl, seen or imagined, can be found on it.

[87] When the re-design of the altar and East wall was planned it was
proposed that the Thornhill *Apotheosis of Chichele* fresco might be transferred to
linen backing, but to save expense this was not done. Sparrow reported that only
fragments 'in very poor condition' survived (Sparrow 1960, p. 6); P. Horden
specifies their number as five and their current location as staircase XIV at the
west end of the Codrington Library (Green & Horden 2007, p. 307). Preparatory
sketches are extant (Sparrow 1960, figs. 2–4) but the 'Green' painting remains
the best illustration of what Shepilinda saw as a whole.

[88] Also by James Thornhill. See Lane Poole 1926, vol. 1, p. 180 (no. IX.2).

[89] The Codrington library buildings, designed by Nicholas Hawksmoor,
were erected between 1716 and 1720. '[In 1721] the College had its library
building; but it was as yet an empty shell, without bookcases. Its great windows
were void of glass and let in wind and rain. The floor was unpaved; the walls
unplastered' (Craster 1971, p. 74). It was to take until 1751 for the interior to be
fully furbished and ready to receive the books (ibid. p. 80).

[90] Shepilinda may have seen the words of *Terrae-Filius* in 1733: 'I would
willingly next pay a Visit to All-Souls, if I could find it out; it us'd to stand on
the Right-Hand above Queen's, but if we may judge from the Resort of its
Members, we should guess it to be translated over the Way, and that the Three
Tuns Tavern was All-Souls College, did not the Effigies of the Good Archbishop
over the Door convince us to the contrary' (Amhurst. 1733, p. 13).

[91] Elizabeth Bradgate took over the running of the Three Tuns Tavern in
High Street after the death of her husband Richard in 1729: J. Haslam, 'Oxford
taverns and the cellars of All Souls in the 17th and 18th Centuries', *Oxoniensia*,
34 (1969), 45–77: he quotes Thomas Hearne's description of her as 'a fine,
stately, beautifull, large young Woman, but very proud & empty of sense, as her
husband also was, and a great Company Keeper': (9 Jan. 1728/9) *Hearne*, vol. 10
(OHS lxvii), 85. Haslam shows that in addition to the Bursar's purchases 'various
Fellows of the College had private accounts with Mrs. Bradgate' (p. 57).

librarian.[92]—There is in the Bookless Library a fine White Marble Statue of Colonel Codrington Some=time fellow of this College who died at Barbadoes[93]—here is a Warden one D[r] Niblet[94] now Vice Can: (but that honour will this Year Slip through his Fat Fingers) he is Married to a fine Wife[95]—who was ever yet a moving Dumpling There are 40 Fellows—but not other Members by reason they Don't care to trouble them=selves with the tutorage of others till they have a Better Command of them=selves—but that must be a work of <u>Time</u>, or I am much mistaken,—The Celebrated D[r] D'oily[96] is of this Fraternity ; & graces it much by his portly presense—this learned D[r] lives (or at lea[st] did) so abstemious a life as not to partake of anima[l] food & yet is the most florid Robust person in Town[.] But it wou'd vex him tho if he knew that people thought him so; for he values himself much upon the

---

[92] The joke about taverns and coffee houses being libraries (because they provided journals, gazettes, directories, etc. for the use of their patrons, and even manuscripts in the form of credit ledgers) is developed at length in *Companion* 1762, pp. 10–13.

[93] Christopher Codrington (1668–1710) was a gentleman commoner at Christ Church from 1685 and was then a Fellow of All Souls from 1690. He inherited his father's West Indies estates in 1699. He lost his Governor Generalship of the Leeward Islands in 1703 and concentrated on his studies and his books, which he left to his college at his death in 1710, together with £10,000 to build the library and buy more books: *ODNB*.

[94] Stephen Niblett (1696–1766, Fellow 1720–6, Warden 1726–66, Vice-Chancellor 1735–8). In the judgement of John Clarke 'he appeared a safe, if somewhat unexciting choice': Green & Horden 2007, p. 219. See also the whole chapter, pp. 217–32. For portraits, both in the Warden's lodgings, see Lane Pool 1926, part 2, pp. 192ff. (IX.42, 43).

[95] Elizabeth née Whitfield (1708–66). Her portrait is in the Warden's lodgings (Lane Pool 1926, part 2, p. 193 (IX.44), the only Warden's wife to be so honoured. There is a joint memorial tablet to the couple in the Chapel (Screech 1997, p. 40).

[96] Foster, *Alumni*: D'Oyley, Thomas, s. Franc. of Chichester, Sussex, gent. Pembroke Coll., matric. 15 Oct., 1724 aged 15; All Souls Coll. B.C.L. 1732, D.C.L. 1737. To be identified with the author of *A sermon preached at St. George's, Hanover Square ... April the 17th, 1766, at the anniversary meeting of the hospitals for the small-pox and inoculation*, by Thomas D'Oyley, LL.D, Archdeacon of Lewes, who was listed as a subscriber living in Kensington Square. Unsurprisingly, his sermon does not mention vegetarianism.

fol. 20r '21'   Whiteness | of his hands, & the Delicacy of his Complexion, this is the only living Curiosity in this College—but if a library without Book[s] & a College without heads[97] may be esteem'd so—this may vie with any in town. The New Building is handsome & over the Iron Gate is a Bust of the Founder; I think I have heard it is a good one, but I am no Judge & all I can say of it is, that it is a Comely white Marble head of a Venerable old Man with a Mitre on—Good Dr Clark[98] whose virtue & generosity is not to be equal'd—gave many Gifts to this College & amongst the rest he gave that fine House the Warden now resides in—which as long as he made this place happy by his life he dwelt in—& had given them much more had not their Worthlessnesses been pleas'd to brand themselves with Ingratitude by denying him a small favour[99] & the only one he ever asked—which made him turn the Scource of his Generosity towards the mean though Worthy Foundation of Worcester College, do you think they were not Justly Served?—In this College they say formerly the Cook turn'd some Ducks loose to be fed with

fol. 20v '22'   the Kitchen Scraps & one of them being | a Mallard was lost for a Considerable time then was found in a sink grown to so large a Size that he cou'd not return & the fattest that ever was heard of—the Fellows all rejoycing at having such a Luscious Bit to liquour their Chops with, thought they could not honour this fat beast of a Bird too much; therefore some of

---

[97]   i.e. (undergraduate) population.

[98]   See above, p. 4, n. 9.

[99]   It is not clear what this request was. Tim Clayton refers only to Clark's exasperation with the deliberate refusal of the conservative majority of the Fellows to agree to the Hawksmoor designs of the buildings to be funded by himself and Philip Wharton (Green & Horden 2007, pp. 128ff.). See also Burrows 1874, p. 384: 'The appeal [to the Visitor] cost the College £700 ... Dr Clarke was so annoyed at the lawsuit that, in the disposition of his munificent bequest to Worcester College he put in a special clause against any Appeal from the election of a Fellow, —"to Visitors or any one else to avoid the shameful and unnecessary expenses which I have seen some Visitors put some Colleges to upon such occasions".'

the Wisest of them composed a Song[100] the Burden of Which was—it was a Swopping, Swapping Malard[101]—(I suppose they had more wit then, then they have now) & one day in the year they have a Malard, & Sing it to the Table with this Song. (for they can Sing tho' they cant write—).

All Souls College was founded in 1437 by Henry Chichely *fol. 21r '23'* Abp of Canterburry that prayers should be there offerr'd up for the Souls that perished in the French War to which he had instigated Henry 5th—Coll: Will: Codrington left a curious collection of Books 4000 pnd to buy more books and 6000 to build a Library—it has a Warden 40 Fellows 2 Chaplains 3 Clerks 6 Choiristers &c—and an August Solemn Chappell. Its lenght[sic] is 144 feet

[UNIVERSITY]

The next College to all Souls is Call'd University & is *fol. 21v '24'* the Benevolent Charity of our Good King Alfred—who in former Days (when Kings were not so uppish) made a friendly Visit to Gillian the Old Sheppherds Wife as Ballad Historyians have told us[102]—here is 2 hansome Quadrangles well built one new the other Something Antique in the new one is the Masters Lodgings which on the outside next to Logick lane resembles a Coffin—in the outward one (which is well Inhabited) Is a Statue of that Venerable (tho merry) Monarch but badly executed—the Chappel is vastly pretty the windows moderatly well painted. in one of them is Jonas

---

[100] The words and the music were recorded by Baskerville and are edited in Quiller Couch 1892, pp. 243–6. (Baskerville 1905, pp. 201–3, omits the music.)

[101] Shepilinda has written 'Swopping, Swopping' and then corrected the second word to 'Swapping'. The authorised text is 'Swapping, Swapping' but one hesitates to accuse her of making nonsense of it.

[102] e.g. 'The Shepherd and the King with *Gillian* the Shepherds Wife, with her churlish answer, being full of mirth and mery pastime'. A transcription of a Glasgow University Library copy (Euing Ballads 332) is available at http://ebba. english.ucsb.edu/ballad/32009/xml (accessed 27 June 2012).

just comming out of the Whales Belly[103] but the painter very
unhappyly Mistook Jonas for the Whale & has made him
much the largest Figure of the two[104]—the hall is a good
hansome room but generally pretty Mucky—this College
has a Master one D[r] Cockman[105] who has for a help Mate[106]
one of the Most extrodinary of her Sex—& is at this time
Nurse & Tutoress to the 2 sons of the Earl of Coventry Viz:
L[d] Deerhurst & M[r] Coventry[107] who are to Copy her in every
thing (a Bright example) I realy pitty the poor Boys heartily &
think it an extream odd[?] thing for 2 young Noble men who are
fol. 22r '25'   suppos'd to make a | Figure in life to be bred up at the Apron
Strings of an Old Woman whose greatest qualifications are
being Mistress of Quadrille, a Curtsey & washing her hands in
the Midle of Dinner Before I take my leave of this Venerable

103 The window was painted and signed by Abraham van Linge in 1641; for
illustrations see Darwall-Smith 2008, pl. 4f (whole windows) and Archer *et al.*,
1988, fig.10, p. 22 (detail). Van Linge had painted the same subject on the East
window of Lincoln chapel ten years earlier.

104 Shepilinda exaggerates: the whale, actually a scripturally correct great
fish, is decisively larger. Moreover, Jonah has completed his exit from its mouth.
See Darwall-Smith 2008, pl. 5.

105 Thomas Cockman came up to Univ. in Jan. 1690/1, and became first a
Browne Exhibitioner in May that year, and then a Bennet Scholar in Feb. 1693/4.
He was elected a Fellow in 1700, resigning his post in 1713. He was elected
Master in 1722, but his election pushed the College into a dispute over the
Mastership which was not fully resolved until 1729. For the whole unedifying
story, see Darwall-Smith 2008, pp. 247–66 (with the faintly comical group
portrait, ibid. pl. 10) [GN] Cockman himself behaved with dignity and restraint
throughout, and, once his position was confirmed beyond dispute in 1729, he
did a remarkable job of healing wounds within the College. He died in 1745.
[RD-S]

106 Mrs Cockman (mentioned again on p. 60) is totally invisible in all records
in the College, so this little glimpse of her is very precious. [RD-S]

107 The sons of Lord Coventry: Thomas Henry Coventry, Lord Deerhurst
and his younger brother, George William, both matric. July 1737, aged 16 and
15 respectively. According to Foster, *Alumni*, both were created M.A.s on 20
Nov. 1739. Thomas was elected M.P. for Bridport in 1742, but died in 1744, and
so George inherited the earldom, and died in 1809. Neither man has an entry in
ODNB, but George's wife Maria does, as 'a figure of scandal' (Coventry [née
Gunning], Maria, Countess of Coventry (baptised 1732, died 1760)). Robert
Eden, one of the College tutors, dedicated his *Jurisprudentia Philologica sive
Elementa Juris Civilis* (1744) to Thomas. [RD-S]

Mansion I must tell you that a Son of Apollo & Nephew of Orpheus[108] has his residence here in the shape of M[r] Richard Brown[109] a Master of arts a favourite of the Muses (who are my Utter Enemies believe me?? Scurvy Jades) endow'd with every Musical accomplishment {of} of his Ilustrious Father & uncle & every other perfection that can make him agreable. besides this Gentleman, I must crave leave to bring one more of this Society (but must take care it be with the utmost gravity) whose name is Marshal,[110] Called by the College the pope; tho as yet has in reality no higher a title then Rector of Maperton[111]—he is a good Man but something Indolent & by his Great deliberation in Speech you wou'd Imagine he labour'd under the Same Infirmity as poor Æsop did before

[108] This probably means no more than that he was an accomplished musician (and possibly singer).

[109] Richard Browne was the only son of Barnabas Browne of St. Martin-in-the-Fields, matric. from Univ. Sept. 1727 aged 14. He was elected a Hearn Exhibitioner in June 1729, and a Bennet Scholar in Mar. 1729/30. He resigned this scholarship at some date before Apr. 1740, having picked up a B.A. in 1731 and an M.A. in 1734. [RD-S]. Volume 1 (Choristers) of Bloxam's exhaustive biographical register of members of Magdalen College has the entry: 'Browne, Richard. Res. 1727. Matr. at Hart Hall, 27 May, 1727, aet. 16. Son of Robert Browne, of St. Peter's, Oxford, pleb. B.A. University College, 10 July, 1731. M.A. July, 1734' (Bloxam 1853, p. 150). Foster, *Alumni* has entries for Richard Brown, son of Robert, matric. from *Hart Hall* in 1727 and eventually held professorships in Arabic and Hebrew; and for Richard Brown, son of *Barnabas*, matric. from *University College*, also in 1727; Foster attaches the Bloxam reference to the second of these despite the forename discrepancy. [RD-S/GN]

[110] John Marshall came up in May 1719 aged 17. He was made a Browne Exhibitioner in Nov. 1719, and then a Bennet Scholar in Apr. 1722. He was elected a Bennet Fellow in May 1729, which post he held until his death in May 1757. He was an active member of the Governing Body, holding most major College offices during the 1730s and 1740s (e.g. he was at various times Bursar, Register, Dean, Librarian and Catechist). [RD-S]

[111] Not Maperton in Somerset (because the Rector there from 1715 to 1766 was Charles Mitchell, famous for conducting a large number of clandestine marriages) but 'Mapperton, a parish in the hundred of Beaminster, division of Bridport, Dorset, standing on an eminence 2 miles from Beaminster, and 136 from London; containing 14 houses and 72 inhabitants. It is a rectory, value 8l. 3s. 1d.' (Capper 1808, s.n.). John Marshall was still Rector in 1756 when he made his will: see Marshall 1883, vol. 1, pp. 172ff.

fol. 22v '26'

he reliev'd the priest[112]—his good Qualifications are very numerous & did not the tenderness of his Constitution hinder him from taking much pains I believe he w^d be Indefaticable ; he is of generous temper & | True to his friend—& a man of Wit & excelent Morals. The Communion Table Cloath is very fine it is a pink Collour'd Silk very richly Embroider'd they know not how they came by it but the Chappell door being left open one night, in the Morning this was found; but notwithstanding all their Ende[avor] the Generous Donor was never discover'd, I have two Couzons Both Gentlemen Commoners of this Colleg[e][113] there is now a vacancy among the Fellows, for Our Admirable B^r Benvolio alias the Revnd Mr Brown[114] is made ArchDeacon of Northampton long may he live to enjoy it——

fol. 23r '27'

University College according to some Authors was founded by King Alfred AD 872 but others reckon it of a more anstient Date & rather esteem King Alfred the Restorer than the Founder of it—the late Famous Dr John Ratcliff[115]

112 The Greek story refers to one or more priestesses of Isis. She/they were recast as a Christian priest or priests in the later European versions, e.g. 'his Person deformed, to the highest degree … he was in a manner Tongue-ty'd too, by such an Impediment in his speech, that People could very hardly understand what he said … There goes a Tradition, that he had the good Hap to relieve certain Priests that were hungry, and out of their Way, and to set them right again; and that for a good Office, he was upon their Prayers, brought to the Use of his Tongue' (L'Estrange 1738, pp. 2ff.). For the ancient version, see Hansen 1998, pp. 106–62.

113 See Introduction, p. xix.

114 John Browne (1687–1764), Master of University Coll. 1744–64, Vice-Chancellor 1750–3. For his identification as Scrippy's brother, see the Introduction, pp. xx, xxi.

115 Foster, *Alumni*: Radcliffe, John, s. George, of Wakefield, Yorks., pleb. University Coll., matric. 23 Mar. 1665/6, aged 15; B.A. 1669: fellow Lincoln Coll., resigned 1677, M.A. 1672, B.Med. 1675. D.Med. 1682, practised in Oxford and in London 1684, physician to Princess Anne of Denmark, fellow College of Physicians 1687, M.P. Bramber 1690–5, and Buckingham 1713–14; died 1 Nov. 1714, buried in St. Mary, Oxford; founded by his will two medical travelling fellowships in University Coll., and further funds from which the Radcliffe Infirmary, Observatory and Library (now Camera) were built. See biographies in Nias 1918, Hone 1950, Guest 1991.

was several years in this house[116] <&> a Member of the Foundation and at his Death left 5000 pounds to build a new front—40 000 pounds to erect a Library and 950 pounds a year for other Publick uses in the University This College has a Master 12 Fellows 10 Scholars 2 exhibitioners The Vice Chancellor Proctors &C are the visitors its length is 250 feet.

[MERTON]

To Merton now I'll take my Journey Scrible a short account *fol. 23v '28'* of it it should be a long one did I know what to say the Gardens are pretty & laid out in agreable Serpentine walks & a very hansome terras with a neat Pavilion[117] at the end of it for the use of the Warden who by the Way is one Dʳ Wyntle[118] one of Dʳ Radcliffs Travelling Phiz's[119] who

---

[116] 'in this house' is written over erased 'a member of'.

[117] This was the warden's summer house, built during the wardenship of Thomas Clayton, 1661–93. 'During Clayton's wardenship, characteristically perhaps, the one building which was added was the summer house at the end of the warden's garden [now absorbed into the fellows' garden], where it commanded a view over the city wall and Christ Church Meadows. Wood naturally considered it a waste of money since the warden already had a fine view over the meadows from the great window at the southern end of his gallery' (Martin & Highfield 1997, p. 215). Wood specifies: 'All which tho unnecessary, yet the poore Coll. must pay for them, and all this to please a woman' [i.e. his wife, Lady Bridget Clayton] (Wood, *Life*, vol. 1, p. 396; see also Brodrick 1885, pp. 112–13 where she is said to have used it to eavesdrop on the Fellows walking along the path to their adjacent garden). Pictured in the Oxford Almanack for 1798 (extreme right): reproduction in Skelton 1823, vol. 2, pl. 98). JR/GN

[118] According to Foster, *Alumni*, Robert Wyntle, son of Richard of the city of Gloucester, gentleman, matric. from Pembroke College, Oxford, 27 Mar. 1699, aged 16. B.A. 1701, fellow of Merton 1705, M.A. 1709, B. and D.Med. 1726. Warden of Merton 1734–50. Radcliffe travelling fellow July 1715. Died 21 Aug. 1750 and buried in Merton chapel. N.B. a Robert, son of Richard Wintle, was baptised at St. Nicholas, Gloucester, 6 Mar. 1681 and Anne, daughter of Richard Wintle, was baptised there on 29 Apr. 1687. (See www.familysearch.org.) [JR]

[119] J. B. Nias received the following information about Wyntle from Warden Brodrick in 1918: 'He was elected Warden July 18, 1734, and died as Warden on 22 Aug. 1750, and was buried in our Chapel. His tenure of office was marked by constant disputes between him and the fellows, which in 1737 were settled,

travell'd much tho profited little & I much fear is a Dunder-
hed but as you find his Caracter you must take it for Bes[s]
won't sputter out all she knows—he has never a Consort
(why who'll have him) his Sister Miss Wyntle[120] is a most
agreable young lady of about 60 years of age her tongue
well hung & does not often freez[e] to the Roof of her
Mouth for want of Motion—in short she is a nymph of
such extensive knowlege that she knows something of
every body & every thing; Moses[121] is a Comoner here the
best natured friendly Man in the College nay in town there
<is> a Namesake of him in the College [erasure] a harmles
kind of an animal Comonly Called Pugg[122]—& now I am
a speaking of the Members I can't forget a Wooley Bear[123]
that Does much honour to the College by inhabiting it &
hinders people from saying as they go by the Gate there

fol. 24r '29'

<is> never a Fellow here of Work & Merit—| of this col-
lege likewise is the Weighty Mr Blythe[124] (wrongly named
for he's just the reverse) a Noble man as wears an Orange
Tawny Gown; I think I said a Man of Weight I meant

at least for a time, by the intervention of the Visitor, Archbishop Potter. I find
that in 1740 he was reprimanded by the Visitor for converting to his own use
£100 placed in his hands for college purposes' (Nias 1918, p. 43).

[120] Anne Wyntle, sister of Robert Wyntle, was buried in Merton chapel
29 Aug. 1746, where there is a mural monument to her erected by her brother.
Robert Wyntle was subsequently buried in the same grave (Bott 1964, pp. 89ff.,
144). She is not mentioned in Martin & Highfield, 1997. [JR]

[121] Unidentified. (No one by surname of 'Moses' at Merton at this date and,
if a forename, very difficult to trace.) [JR]

[122] Unidentified. [JR]

[123] Presumably Samuel Woolley, son of Richard Woolley of Worcester,
gentleman, matric. from Trinity College 11 Mar. 1716/17 aged 16. B.A. 1720,
M.A. from Merton 1723, prebendary of Worcester 1760, died 5 Nov. 1764.
Appears in college records as both Woolley and Wolley; in Foster, *Alumni* under
Wolley. He may have been admitted fellow of Merton *c.* 1721 but undocumented
so far. [JR]

[124] No 'Blythe' at Merton, but John Bligh, son of John, Earl of Darnley,
matric. from Merton 13 May 1735 as a Gentleman Commoner, aged 15, and was
created M.A. 13 July 1738. He would fit the description of 'Noble man'; he was the
only Gentleman Commoner on the books at that date to be given the honorific
'The Honble'. Subsequently 3rd Earl of Darnley. Died 31 July 1781. [JR]

Bulk, for he{s}'s of the largest size; a great Unhavourly[125] Cub; I'm sure he'd like to have sat in my lap at the Consort Apelles[126] says he's Bashfull, but I must say I think him the reverse; for I never saw a greater nor more awkward asurance in my life but he's too insignificant a subject for my sweet pen; there's a complement to my self now—the Quadrangle[127] is pretty enough & so[128] the Fellows think for they take it all up themselves & leave all {you} Young Members to scrap for themselves, there has lately been a Visitation here but it is not determin'd yet[129]—NB the Warden sometimes swears that's wrong; I think Mr Shute[130] was formerly an accomplish'd Fellow of this house; but resign'd it in favour of a Most Agreable Wife; he has lately compos'd a Concerto de Rumbello——

Merton College has for its Founder Walter BP of Roch- *fol. 24v '30'* ester who 1ˢᵗ planted this Society at Maldon in Surrey AD 1264 from whence he translated it to Oxford in 1267 The Chappel which is also the Parish Church of Sᵗ John the

---

[125] This word of Shepilinda's own coining recurs as a derogatory description of the Muses on p. 82. It apparently means 'unmannerly'. (*OED* has *havour* as alternative to *haviour* and notes that sixteenth- century *havour*, beside its original sense of 'possession', took also that of *behavour* [later *behaviour*], but it has no derivative with *ly*.)

[126] Presumably an acquaintance either called Painter or actually a painter. If the former then probably John Painter, matric. from St. John's 1733, aged 17, B.A. 1737.

[127] Fellows' Quadrangle, previously called the Great Quadrangle. Commissioned by Henry Savile, Warden 1585–1622. Built 1608–10 to provide improved accommodation for fellows, who had previously lived in Mob (Little) Quad. See Bott 1993, pp. 37–9. [JR]

[128] '& so' is written over erased 'but'.

[129] Wyntle had a reputation for being both domineering and a reformer. He quickly fell out with several of the fellows after his election and sought a visitation of the college by its Visitor, John Potter, Archbishop of Canterbury, which took place in the summer of 1738. See for a full account Martin & Highfield 1997, pp. 248–55. [JR]

[130] Presumably Christopher Shute, son of Nathaniel of Cheverell, Wilts., clergyman, matric. from Trinity College 6 June 1717 aged 15. B.A. 17 Feb. 1720/21; M.A. from Merton 1724. Admitted fellow of Merton 8 Oct. 1723; resigned his fellowship 1 Aug. 1737. [JR]

Baptist is a Splendid Building the Inner Quadrangle[131] is
very Beautifull This College has a Warden 20 Fellows 14
Portionists (now called post Masters)[132] &C: & is famous for
a well furnish'd library & a delightfull Garden The Visitor
is the Abp of Canterbury its length is 255 feet.

[CORPUS CHRISTI]

fol. 25r '31'   Corpus Christi College is the nearest to that I last mention'd
This Colleg is now Govern'd by the president one D^r
Mather[133] a personage very little Better than an Old Woman
The College is pretty, small, and neat, in the Midle of the
Quadrangle stands a Dial the most extrodinary one I ever
saw for I defy the very Pope himself Unless he is a very
good mathematician to know what a clock it is by it any
hour of the Day[134] They never had any Curiosity's in this
College but one; which was their founders Mitre; but they
fearing to be thought old Musty antiquarians sold it for 90

---

[131] Mob Quad, previously Little Quad. Arguably the oldest quad in Oxford,
built between *c.* 1288 and 1378. The old (medieval) library occupies the first
floor of the west and south ranges. This quad originally housed the fellows.
After they transferred to the Great/Fellows' Quad post 1610, it was occupied by
undergraduates and B.A.s, which possibly gave it its name. See Bott 1993, pp.
16–23. [JR]

[132] *Postmaster* is the Merton term for a Scholar. [JR]

[133] Mather, John, son of William of Manchester, pleb., matric. from Christ
Church 21 Mar. 1692/3, aged 16. Scholar of Corpus Christi 1693 [22 Dec.
according to Fowler 1893]. B.A. 1696, M.A. 22 Feb. 1699/1700. Probationary
Fellow 1704; B.D. 1708; D.D. 9 Mar. 1714/15. President 1715–48; Vice-
Chancellor 1723–8. Rector of Helmdon, Northants., 1723. Died 15 Apr. 1748
[Foster]. Married 19 Apr. 1715 Rebecca Pococke at St. Andrew's, Chinnor. Had
at least eight children. According to Hearne (12 Jan. 1714/15) in vol. 5 (OHS
xlii), 15, 'This Morning Mr John Mather was elected President of Corpus. He
is a very honest, good-natured, ingenious man, and hath published two or three
sermons.' See Fowler 1893, p. 277. [JR]

[134] The Pelican Sundial designed by Charles Turnbull, author of *A Perfect and
Easie Treatise of the Use of the Celestiall Globe* (1585), in the late sixteenth century.
The date of its erection is usually given as 1581. See Pattenden 1979, p. 100;
Pattenden 1980, p. 52. The sundial actually has nine separate dials (that I can
count). [JR]

pounds to build 6 rooms for Gentlemen Commoners;[135] they all being professors of Modern politenes; they have a little bit of a garden here. NB no Women Bedmakers here[136] The new Buildings are all screen'd from the Sun, in order to preserve the Complexions of the Young Gentlemen who in all probabilty sitting so long as they do to studdy in a rome where Phoebus came, might be Tann'd Good Natured M[r] Leigh Masters,[137] is a Gentleman Commoner here Scrip and I are his Tutoresses[138] | Mr Fosset[139] of this College Master *fol. 25v '32'*

[135] See Fowler 1893, pp. 280–1: a new building for the college's six Gentleman Commoners was built *c*. 1734–5 (limited to six in Founder's statutes). The Tower Book (in which were recorded deposits into and payments out of the treasury) entry for 21 Dec. 1736 records, 'The Mitre being so much decayed and broken that it could not be mended and put together again, it was agreed to sell it and a few old battered pieces of silver ... for £96–16–6.' [JR]

[136] No women allowed in college by the Founder's statutes, which prohibited the laundresses from coming beyond the lodge (Fowler 1893, p. 49). Female bed-makers had been allowed in after the Restoration (ibid. p. 50) but were then forbidden by Visitor's statute in 1678 following the Matthew Curtois case (ibid. p. 253). [JR/GN]

[137] Foster, *Alumni*: Legh Master, son of Legh of St. George's, Queen Square, armiger. Matric. from Corpus Christi 16 Dec. 1737 aged 20; later of New Hall, Lancs., and of Codnor Castle, Derbs. Died in America in 1796. Inherited Codnor and Newhall on father's death, 1750. Either 'good natured' is being used ironically or his behaviour at the time belied his true character. A search for 'Legh Master' online produces rather a lot of hits for him, revealing a very unpleasant character. He set up as an ironmaster in Maryland using slave labour. Nothing unusual for the time, except that he killed two of his slaves, one for refusing his sexual advances, and the other for trying to defend her. He also abandoned his wife and daughter during the American War of Independence. The ground where he was first buried is supposed to have rejected his body, and his ghost is now supposed to haunt the graveyard where he was eventually buried. However, there is little doubt that the atrocity stories grew *pari passu* with the alleged haunting and supernatural appearances. The article quoted in the next note gives a judicious account, noting, for instance, that 'It is quite possible that the slave Sam simply ran away', and concludes 'Leigh Master should not be judged too harshly he was the victim, some historians assert, of the ignorant and superstitious'. [JR/GN]

[138] This is unclear but may be linked to the preceding 'Good Natured' and construed to mean that he is good natured *as a result of* the women's tutoring. In America 'Leigh Masters was known as "a rough man" in manners no uncommon thing in the early days' (*The Gettysburg Times*, Fri. 11 Mar. 1966, p. 10). [GN]

[139] Richard Fawcett, son of John Fawcett of the city of Durham, armiger, matric 26 Aug. 1730, aged 15. B.A. 1734; M.A. 7 Feb. 1737/8; Probationary

of Arts is a very pretty young Gentleman & plays finely upon y[e] Harpsicord

Corpus Christi College Founded AD 1516[140] By R[d] Fox Bp of Winton[141] Privy Councelour & L[d] Privy Seal to Henry y[e] 7th & 8 it hath[142] a President 20 Fellows 20 Scholars & two Chaplains &c. The first Court is an Antient regular handsome Building The Library Contains a noble treasure of Books—The Garden is small but kept neat and in good order—but the most splendid part of this College is a Stately Row of Lodgings to the South erected by the late president D[r] Turner[143] the Bp of Winton Visitor———

[ORIEL]

fol. 26r '33' Oriel[144] I'll now describe at least endeavour so to do & I fancy I shall not have a very Dificult task—The College is Built in parts not regular pretty enough The provost is D[r] Hodges;[145] his lodgings are good enough but inconvenient: furnish'd well enough for an Elderly Batchelor—there are a

Fellow 1738; B.D. 1745; D.D. 1748. Vicar of Newcastle, rector of Gateshead and prebendary of Durham. Died 22 Apr. 1782. [JR]. He appears in stanza 5 of the poem 'Upon our Rare Consort' (p. 86). See the note added there.

140 The charter of foundation was signed by the founder on 1 Mar. 1516/17 and the first President and fellows were put in possession of the college on 5 Mar. See Fowler 1893, pp. 57–8.

141 Shepilinda seems to have written Rgd (for Reginald?) but Richard Fox, 1447/8–1528, Bishop of Winchester, must be meant and appears in Baskerville (see above, p. xxiv). For the life of Richard Fox, see *ODNB*.

142 For the exeptional *hath* rather than *has*, see Introduction, p. xxiv.

143 See Fowler 1893, pp. 261–72. Thomas Turner, born 20 Sept. 1645, son of Thomas Turner, Dean of Canterbury [although, at this time ejected and resident in Bristol]. Admitted scholar 6 Oct. 1663. Probationary Fellow 24 Dec. 1672. Elected President 13 Mar. 1687/8. Died 29 Apr. 1714. Had built, at his own expense, between 1706 and 1712, the neoclassical building that faces south over the college garden. Originally called the Turner Building, now called the Fellows' Building. [JR]

144 I thank Robert Petre, Oriel archivist, and Paul Seaward for help with this section. See Catto 2013, chapters 6 to 8.

145 Walter Hodges (1676–1757), Dean 1722–3, 1734–5, Provost 1727–57, Vice-Chancellor 1742–4.

good many Fellows; one of them Viz: D[146] Fisher is librarian—here is instead of a Garden a Grass plot a small Terras & a fine Pomgranet Tree at the end of it. Whose fruit is Delicious as they Tell me but I dont know that for Certain, for I had it from no one but the provost. in this college shines the Gold Tuft of L[d]. Wenman,[147] & the Genteel M[r]. Talbot[148] & the most deserving Young Gentleman I know; M[r] Talbot is a Gentleman[149] Commoner throwoly[sic!] well bred Genteel & polite, without Afectaition[sic]; Modest without reserve, & Gay without Galoping | Generous without extravagance *fol. 26v '34'* in short to sum up his Character in few words as posible I will only add he is what every True English Gentleman of Fortune ought to be—his B[r] is a Commoner[150] & very deserveing but Shines not quite with so Radiant a Lustre as his Elder B[r] L[d] Wenman I should have said more of & now will say few of our Young Nobility are so Courteous Sober & affable a Man of very solid Sense a great Oeconomist & a Good Scholar; & if he lives will make if not a great, what is much Better, & that is a good Man ; there is no very great Curiosity in this College except D[r] Edmonds[151] D[r] of Law a Man that talks as much as 3 women. [NB] all that I have said of M[r] Talbot is litterally true; but comes as far short of his Inimitable Character; as the patcht Coat of a labourer does to the Duke of Lorains best wedding Coat[152]———

[146] Robert Fysher (1699 ?), Christ Church 1715–29, Dean 1727–8. Fellow and Bodley's Librarian 1729–47, Treasurer 1728–9, 1729–30, 1736–7, 1744–5.

[147] Philip, Viscount Wenman (d. 1760). Matric. 1737.

[148] Charles Talbot, Lord Talbot. Matric. 1702.

[149] The present editor inadvertently omitted the MS. line 'I know; M[r] Talbot is a Gentleman' from the transcription supplied to Paul Seaward and quoted by him (Catto 2013, p. 238). Apologies are here expressed for the resulting confusion between the brothers in this passage.

[150] Mr Edward Talbot, brother of Charles. Resigned to marry in 1715.

[151] Dr. Henry Edmunds, one of the five elected Fellows whom the Provost refused to admit. See Paul Seward in Catto 2013, pp. 173ff.

[152] The Holy Roman Emperor Francis I (1708–65) was Duke of Lorraine from 1728 to 1737 and married Maria Theresa, daughter of the Emperor Charles VI, in 1736. Several portraits of the Duke wearing an elaborately braided and colourful coat were painted and copies of these were made. (Joseph Highmore 1692–1780

fol. 27r '35'   Oriel College, The Honour of Founding the College is ascribed <to> King Edward the 2nd tho' he did little more towards it, then impower Adam de Brome his Almoner to Build and endow a College: who was a sedulous promoter, & generous contributer towards it. King Edward the 3^d^ gave le Oriel Tenement to this Society on which ground the College so named now stands; It consist<s> of a handsome regular Quadrangle; it has a Provost 18 Fellows 12 exhibitioners &c: The Bp of Lincoln is Visitor it<s> length is 161 feet.

[WADHAM]

fol. 27v '36'   Wadham College I shall next take a walk to. & tell you there is a Warden one Dr Thistlethwaite;[153] a Humdrum sort of an Animal, tho' not a very Harmless one—he has a She Manciple,[154] in whom he much delights & keeps a Chariot for her to air her Carcase in (need enough) he has some Fellows, & sure this ought to be an[155] agreable Society when the Fellows & Warden are of the Same Small Capacity[156]

painted the Duke's portrait from memory, according to Hobbes 1849, p. 199a.)

153 Robert Thistlethwaite (1690?–1744), Warden 1724–39, was an active and predatory homosexual. In Feb. 1739 he was accused of an assault on an undergraduate, resigned the Wardenship and fled to Boulogne. Among his targets were also the college servants (barber, butler, etc.). Shepilinda's account is interesting in that it shows that his proclivities were apparently well known before the actual scandal. For details, see *ODNB*, and Sutherland & Mitchell 1986, p. 350. For contemporary sources, see above all the entertaining, sensationalist, but, as far as I can see, largely accurate account in Anonymous 1739a ('A Faithful narrative . . .'). There is also the burlesque poem Anonymous 1739b ('College-wit sharpen'd . . .'). [CD]

154 The manciple was responsible for obtaining provisions for a college. Shepilinda is an intelligent observer and realises that this manciple is an object of 'delight' and a 'She' to the Warden (who has provided him with the use of a carriage). The 'Faithful narrative' records that it was the Manciple who was sent to fetch William French (matric. 1736 aged 19) to the Warden's Lodgings where he was abused (Anonymous 1739a, p. 2). [GN] The name of this manciple, known to have held office at least between 1730 and 1752, was Richard Harris (variously spelled), and he seems to have extricated himself successfully from the Thistlethwaite scandal. [CD]

155 Written over struck out 'agr' and only partly legible. [GN]

156 That the college was at a low ebb at the time is pretty well agreed.

but instead of that they are making out the old Proverb the Members of the same trade cant agree. The College is pretty enough; in the end Window of the Hall is painted in the Glass their Foundress Dame Dorothy Wadham, well done[157]—the Warden has a very pretty Garden but I never saw it, for as the Head of this College cant marry,[158] no ladies walk here to shew them selves—| The Chapell is a *fol. 28r '37'* pretty place enough all paved with Black & white Marble but no decorations[159]—thats all I have to say of this College

———

Wadham College was finish'd by Dorothy the Relict of Nicholas Wadham who first design'd it AD. 1610. This College has a large regular beautifull Quadrangle. The Windows of the Chappell which is a Building that stands out behind the Quadrangle to the East regularly-answering to the library are finely painted[160] its Garden is large[161] hand-somely laid out & very pleasant The Bp: of Bath & Wells is the Visitor its length is 177 feet.

For instance, when the scandal blew up there was only one fellow actually in residence. [CD]

[157] The windows in the end wall of the hall were replaced in the mid-Victorian period and the glass picture of Dorothy Wadham was moved. Assuming a portrait roundel rather than a full-length portrait is meant we can refer to the mention by Jackson of medallions of Charles I, Henrietta Maria, and Dorothy in the buttery passage (Jackson 1893, p. 190). He also mentions oval medallions of Founder and Foundress in the east window of the Old Library (ibid. p. 197), which are still in place. The medallion portrait of Dorothy Wadham is illustrated as the frontispiece to Davies & Garnett 2009. [CD/GN]

[158] The reference to the Wardens not being allowed to marry is the result of a peculiarity of the original statutes, and remained in force until an act of Parliament of 1806. [CD]

[159] The early nineteenth-century watercolour reproduced in Davies & Garnett 2009, p. 137 shows in essence what Shepilinda saw, including the black and white marble floor. [GN]

[160] The tailpiece gives Shepilinda a chance to mention the Chapel again, this time to praise the impressive 1622 van Ling East Window (Davies & Garnett 2009, p. 138).

[161] The gardens were even more extended from 1795. [CD]

[NEW][162]

fol. 28v '38'   Now for the College of Colleges New College I mean; in this Sweet mansion is every thing agreable—the Garden[163] is elegant the Mound is very high & is a Considerable ornament; at the Botto[m] of which grow two Yew Trees the finest I ever saw cut in Square Pillars of a vast heigth; behind the Mount is a Sweet Walk in which the most peircing Beams of the Sun could never yet penetrate—between the Mount & the Iron Gates & Pallisadoes that Seperate the College from the Garden are four parterres; in one is a Dial laid out in Box which once in a day goes right—in another Parterre which answers that, is something I dont know what though—in the third is the Kings arms blazond properly with particoulour'd Gravells & smiths Cinders enclos'd with Box with the Garter motto round it in the fourth & last parterre is the founders W^m of Wichams arms which are 3 red Roses blazon'd properly with the

fol. 29r '39' | Same Materials as that I last mention'd & round it the Motto Manners Maketh Man[164]—which good precept is Follow'd by most of the Members of the College especially the polite Mr Dobson[165]—the Chapell is very Fine the Windows Curiously painted but by the long course of

---

[162] The text and notes for this section have previously appeared online. See Introduction, p. xxix.

[163] For a near-contemporary illustration, see the 1732 print by William Williams reproduced in Buxton 1976, p. [5]. The mount, however, is clearer in Loggan's view of 1675 (Buxton 1976, front cover). [GN]

[164] Compare a 1684 account of the garden, from Bodleian MS. Rawl. D 810 (Baskerville the antiquarian), fol. 21r: 'Some new building are [*sic*] now erecting on the Eastside of this College, and they have in their Garden 4 Curious knots of Box in severall quarters, in which are cut, the Kings Arms, ye College Arms, the Founders Arms & a Diall. Here is also cast up in this garden, a fair mount & on the top on't to which you ascend by winding walks [text 'walls'] a diall resembling a bundle of Books' (Baskerville 1905, pp. 191ff.).

[165] William Dobson, LLB. He is best known now for having translated Milton's *Paradise Lost* into Latin verse and published it in two handsome volumes (Oxford University Press, 1750). It was commissioned by William Benson the politician and architect, who reputedly paid Dobson £1000 for it (*ODNB*, s.n. 'Benson, William'). [WP]

time they have been there the Coulours are sunk 2 of them
have been lately revived & by Judges of painting are Said
to be very accurately Done & so they had need for the<y>
Cost a hundred pounds a Window[166]—<T>here is a very
fine organ here[167] the Organist M‍ʳ Richard Church[168] who
plays well; Mince[169] the Quirister sings here sweetly; Scrip
& I went up the Mathematical Stairs[170] Into the organ loft
where M‍ʳ Church play'd an Anthem & Mince sang; then
our Scrip sat down like a Fairy Queen in a Cowslip & she
sang & play'd most harmoniously—but hold I was going
to break of a little abruptly & not tell you what a fine
Bowling green there is, Most nicely kept; & overlook'd
by Edmund Hall[171]—| you must know the Fellows Bowl *fol. 29v '40'*

[166] For the agreement between 'Mr William Price of Kirby Street, Hatton
Garden, Glass Painter, his Executors or Assigns on the one part & John Coxed,
Warden of St. Mary College of Winchester in Oxford commonly calld. New
College', dated 4 Dec. 1736, see Woodforde 1951, pp. 16–18. Work started on
the south side of the Choir, and the agreed cost was £63 a window, with a £21
bonus if the work was completed within a given time. Price was indeed paid
£84 per window for his first five, replaced between 27 June 1735 and 16 Sept.
1740. [WP]

[167] Built by Robert Dallam in 1662–3; Dallam was interred in the Cloisters
where his skill in making the *instrumentum pneumaticum quod vulgò nuncupatur
organum* can still be easily discerned on the floor a few metres after one turns
right from the entrance. Dallam received £443 12s 7d for his work; the case cost
a further £162 12s, and its decoration £100 (Buxton & Williams 1979, p. 270).
[WP]

[168] Richard Church was appointed organist in 1732, and held his post for
45 years. He 'was esteemed a good musician, but not a very brilliant player'
(Buxton & Williams 1979, p. 273). [WP]

[169] 'Mince', otherwise untraced, must have been one of the sixteen statutory
choristers. Note the Quirister / Cho(i)rister spellings in this account: the former
is still used at Winchester College. Compare MS. Eng. Poet. f 6, fol. 26r, on the
death of a New College 'Coyrister', a hint at the older pronunciation? [WP]

[170] Seemingly so called because of their minuscule depth: see the letter from
Horace Walpole to Lady Ossory, 9 Sept. 1783, deploring the Reynolds window
and also referring to the organ loft stairs being so narrow that 'not having broken
my neck I can almost believe I could dance a minuet on a tight rope': copy in
New Coll. Archives, PA/SMA 10/3. [WP]

[171] Laid out in the early seventeenth century: see the Latin elegiacs written
by a fellow in 1633 into the endpapers of the printed book, now New College
BT 1.130.9 (commencing with the first edition of More's *Utopia*), 'Haec ego
ter quinis memini mutarier annis / Aedibus Oxoniae Wiccame clare tuis'. The

here to get them stomachs to relish their 12 & 6 a Clock Comons[172]—This College is govern'd by a Youngish kind of a Warden one D[r] Coxhead[173] who has lately taken unto him a fine fat Wife with a great Fortune[174] I fancy he hopes to be Warden of Winchester[175] My Cozen Mill[176] is a Gentleman Comoner of this College his lodgings are pretty & neat; only he wants a Scutching[177] to one of his Cupboard locks, which my Cozen Philadelphia[178] & I pulled of—Mr Harris[179] of this College loves Cold Duck & Cucummers for breakfast; and Mr Speed[180] is a good natured Man—I fancy

writer recalls that 'Si laudas globis area lata patet', surely a reference to a new bowling green (now the lawn to the south of the Mound). [WP]

[172] See Introduction, note 53.

[173] John Coxed, Warden 1730–4; see Buxton & Williams 1979, pp. 228–9 on the refurbishment of the chapel in his time. [WP]

[174] This was Cecilia, daughter of Isaac Selfe, of Beanacre, who was previously married to Ezekiel Wallis from Lucknam, near Chippenham, Wilts. She was aunt to Paul Methuen who purchased Corsham Court in 1747, so the 'great Fortune' was not exaggerated. She died in 1759. See *Wiltshire Notes and Queries*, vol. 5 (1908), 382. [GN]

[175] As indeed he became 1740–57, as was conventional; the wardenship of Winchester was considerably more lucrative than that of New College. [WP]

[176] Mill is Richard Mill, matric. 15 Feb. 1734/5, aged 18, the son of Richard Mill baronet of Woolbeding in West Sussex (Commoners List indexed from New Coll. Archives, CA 3058). [WP] Foster, *Alumni* gives matriculation date as 17 Feb. and adds: created M.A. 12 July 1738, 6th baronet, M.P. Hampshire 1765–88, died 17 Mar. 1770.

[177] Shepilinda undoubtedly means the *escutcheon*, the brass keyhole plate. This form is not found elsewhere and it is likely that she had heard it (from a craftsman?) but not seen it written. [GN]

[178] Philadelphia Mill who died unmarried in 1782. See Dallaway 1815, chart on p. 233. [GN]

[179] Either John Harris who matriculated in 1723 (fellow 1725–38), William who matriculated in 1725 (fellow 1729–59), or Richard who matriculated in 1729 (fellow 1731–48) (see New Coll. Archives, Sewell's register, pp. 241, 242, 244 respectively [Sewell: *Registrum Custodum, Sociorum et Scholarium Collegii Novi*]. In 1738 William (not John, as one would expect from the date) donated to the library several books including an incunable of Terence (ibid. Benefactors Book, p. 167). [WP]

[180] Foster, *Alumni*: Speed, Samuel, s. John, of Southampton, Hants., doctor. New Coll., matric. 30 Nov. 1723, aged 18; B.A. 1727, M.A. 1731, rector of Martyr Worthy and Ludshelfe, Hants., 1755, preb. of Chichester 1739, and of Lincoln 1746.

the Hall of this College is fine tho' I never saw it; but as it belongs here, it must be fine———

New College was founded by William of Wickham Bp: of Winchester in 1386. The Society have within some years past made great improvements to the Buildings Their Chappell is very Solemn & splendid & at the end of it is their hall which answers to the Magnificence of the Buildings they have a lofty Tower, with a Ring of 10 Bells in it;[181] a Library well furnisht with Books ; & a garden laid out in a curious form. This College has a Warden 70 Fellows and S[c]holars; 10 Chaplains 3 Clerks 16 Choiristers—The Visitor is the B^p: of Winchester

fol. 30r '41'

[QUEEN'S]

The next thing I present you with Scrippy is a queen encaged[182] (now taken by Serjeant Death & enshrined) which gives name to a fine regular Built College ; her late Majesty gave something or other to pay the labourers with, that Built it; what her donation was I know not; but I fancy not very liberal[183] & had not Grim Death fetched her away she had given them some more ; this College wou'd take me up a long series of Time were I Carefully to observe each beauty of it ; the Chappell is an admirable fair structure The east end

fol. 30v '42'

---

[181] Five bells were turned into eight first of all: see the late seventeenth-century poem 'On the Bells of new colledge in Oxon lately were molded; and from 5 were turn'd into Eight', MS. Rawl. poet. 84, fols. 105r–104r (reading retrograde): see the transcription online in the *New College Notes* article 'The Bells of New College, from Five to Eight to Ten' (http://www.new.ox.ac.uk/new-college-notes). The last two bells were early eighteenth-century additions. [WP]

[182] The 'queen encaged' refers to the cupola over the High Street entrance which houses the statue by Henry Cheere of Queen Caroline, wife of George II (see above, p. 4, n. 12; Magrath 1921, vol. 1, pp. 93ff. with pl. xli; Tyacke 1998, p. 155. This was a recent addition having only been finished in 1733–4 and Caroline died in 1737.

[183] She had, in fact, given £1000 towards the building, so it was fairly liberal! [MR] See Magrath, vol. 1, p. 92. The money was obtained by Provost Smith (see note 198 below).

of it is in an oval form ; the Windows painted pretty well:
especialy that of the Ascension; the Carved work & Cieling
are fine & kept very neat—The Library is hansome & well
furnish'd with Books but all except the Treatises concerning
<u>Logick</u>[184] are grown a small matter Mouldy. this{,} Foundation
is not for Gentlemen:[185] & they are generally Cumberland &
Northumberland Folks ; they were formerly a very unpolish'd
Set of people but are now grown a much more[186] polite Body
for they were Boots now; nay of late days they wear leather
ones: instead of the Straw Thrums they had used to bedeck
fol. 31r '43' their leggs with, to keep the cold & wet out; | in the Library
was formerly a Most Curious piece of penmanship of the
Devils':[187] but at present it is not visible; the Changeable
Dr Shaw[188] M^r <u>Vice</u> Provost having taken possession of it
to preserve so Delicate an antique from being tatter'd &
torn & defil'd by the Snuffy thumbs & fingers of Illiterate
persons—the Fellows that dine at the high table {Sit at the
High Table} Sit all with their Backs against the Wall & the

---

[184] i.e. the course books required by second- and third-year undergraduates.
See Godley 1908, pp. 56ff.

[185] The barb about gentlemen comes about because the college had for
several centuries been almost exclusively for men from Cumberland and
Westmorland. [MR]

[186] Written over erased 'better'.

[187] Not a manuscript (!) but a woodcut illustration in a printed book. It was
seen by von Uffenbach in 1710: 'The person who was showing us the [Queen's]
library wished to point out something very remarkable a paper said to have
been written by the devil himself. He brought to us the following curious
book: *Ambrosii ex Comitibus Albonesii Introductio in Chaldaicam Linguam, Syriacam,
atque Armenicam & decem alias linguas, Papiae,* 1539: where at folio 193b. is an
appendix multarum diversarumque Linguarum, in which appear many alphabets in
woodcut. In this appendix is also found at fol. 212 b. *Ludov. Spoletani praecepta,
sive, ut vulgo dicitur, conjuratio cum subscripta Daemonis responsione.* It was at that
time superstitiously declared that on the use of this incantation an apparition
appeared which threw down a paper with the accompanying words. The letters
resemble those of the Chinese alphabet': von Uffenbach 1928, pp. 7ff. The page
is conveniently reproduced in Wood, *Life,* vol. 1, pl. VII (facing p. 498).

[188] Thomas Shaw (1694–1751) fellow from 1727, elected FRS 1734, Principal
of St. Edmund Hall and Regius Professor of Greek. His changeability is probably
a reference to his travelling. See below, p. 45 and notes, and *ODNB.* [MR]

poor Children, or Tabiters[189] that wait on them, stand with
their Faces towards them, & their 2 thumbs across upon the
table[190]—which custom has been ever Since one of them
Stab'd a person in the time of Diner or Super I don't know
which but my Memory won't let me tell you who it was, how
it was, nor when it was, But thus much I believe that true it
was; across the lower end of the hall runs a Gallery (but Stay
I Shoud first have told you That the Hall is a very hansome
lofty Room & at the upper end is a very fine Beautiful ~~Pictur~~
Picture of Queen Philippa;[191] & another of Robert Eccles-
field[192] her Conffessor or prime | Minister I cant tell which)   *fol. 31v '44'*
as looks down into the hall[193] where Scrip & I saw them{e}[194]
dine & once I saw them Sup—out of the Gallery you go
into the Common room; where our Scrip Poked the fire for
them; there is a Good Hospitable Grate & a handsome Marble

---

[189] The taberdars or poor boys were once young boys given a basic education,
but by the eighteenth century were B.A.s who were effectively scholars who
were kept on the foundation until they could become fellows (one had to be an
M.A. to be a fellow). It therefore seems very unlikely that they served at table,
and I think she is probably confusing the taberdars with some undergraduates
who did pay their way by serving at table. I have not heard the story of the
thumbs before. [MR]

[190] Similarly Baskerville: 'In this Colledge some tell me, at meals they sit
at table or tables in their Hall with backes against yᵉ wall or wainscot and their
faces looke all one way. The reason why they do so, some say was this. One
of their Society being killed by a stab in yᵉ back, when eating at a Table in the
Hall they do to prevent the like evills sit as I said with their faces all looking
forward one way' (p. 221). Magrath 1921, vol. 2, p. 97 (with n. 2) comments:
'She is probably mixing up the disputations at table, prescribed in Eglesfield's
Statutes, with the practice during the drinking of the loving cup for the person
on each side of the drinker to stand up for his protection. No one was to sit on
the opposite side of the table' (see Magrath vol. 1, pp. 54ff. with n. 8 there, and
supplementary note p. 359: 'the prohibitions as to sitting on the opposite side
of the table have been neglected since about 1862').

[191] Lane Poole 1926, vol. 1, p. 110 (no. VI.7), by Thomas Murray.

[192] Lane Poole 1926, vol. 1, p. 108 (no. VI.1), also by Thomas Murray. Given
by a different donor fifteen years earlier than the portrait of the Queen.

[193] The hall is still laid out as described, with Philippa and Eglesfield (her
chaplain) in pride of place, as is the Common Room off the gallery (though
there are no pipes any more!). [MR]

[194] Or 'the me<n>'

Chimney piece; the Beaufet[195] Is well Stock'd with nutmegs
pipes tobacco Wax Candle & every other Utensil fitt for topers
& Smoakers with which this foundation abounds—they have
no Garden but a very handsome large Bowling Green, with
Statues in Niches, which I took for kings & Queens: but was
told by a Comoner that they were the 12 apostles: Which as
he said So, I was Obliged to believe; though I never heard
there were any Women apostles before[196]—there is a fine well
paved Cloister which goes quite round the new Building (a
pretty place to walk in the wet in especialy for your White
Stockings Beauxs, who fear Dirt & Wind—there is many
such here) Mʳ Low[197] at the head of them who is Sorely Smit-
ten, & bit with loves Passion to a Vast degree but I won't Say

fol. 32r '45'   to who, least I disgrace him. ^{That was well ?barred?}. | This College
shou'd be govern'd by the Provost one Dr Smith;[198] but here
the Grey Mare is the Better horse[199]—so she governs him

---

[195] Buffet, sideboard.

[196] The statues on the west side of the Library are not the apostles, but
are Sir Joseph Williamson, Archbishop Lamplugh, Bishop Barlow, Robert de
Eglesfield, Edward III, Philippa of Hainhault, Charles I and Henrietta Maria.
They look out over what was then the Fellows' Garden and is now the Provost's
Garden. [MR] See Magrath 1921, vol. 2, p. 97 (with n. 3) quoting Shepilinda.
(We note how she hides her contempt for her informant's ignorance or malice
behind mock naivety and trust.) [GN].

[197] Foster, *Alumni*: 'Lowe, Samuel, s. Samuel, of Southwell, Notts., arm.
Queen's Coll., matric. 14 May, 1736, aged 17; died in Aug. 1765, ancestor of
Lord Sherbrooke'. He married Elizabeth, daughter and co-heiress of Henry
Sherbrooke of Oxton Hall in 1740, and it must be the courtship leading to that
marriage about which Shepilinda is being coy.

[198] Joseph Smith (1670–1756). See *ODNB*. Matric. from Queens in 1689,
Senior Proctor in 1704 and became known as 'Handsome Smith' to distinguish
him from his junior colleague 'Thomas Smith'. Having refused to stand for the
provostship in 1704 he was elected to it in 1730. In the interim he had pursued
his career in London in the Church, at Court, and in theological controversy,
and had married Mary Lowther in 1709. He used his contacts to obtain the large
grant from Queen Caroline (above, note 183) and was a reforming provost who
endeavoured to raise standards. [MR/GN]

[199] 'grey mare is the better horse' (=the wife rules the husband)' (Wilson 1970,
p. 338a). If Shepilinda is correct some at least of the credit for Smith's success
must go to Mary. [GN]

& Rules the College; one son[200] God has bless'd them with,
who wears Silk shoes. I supose to make his heels as light as
his head is empty—The Vice Provost (as I told you before) is
D[r] Shaw,[201] a Great Virtuosa & has brought many Curiositys
with him out of Egypt: I never hear'd why he went there,[202]
but I know he has wrote an acount of his travels,[203] & publish'd
it by Subscription; he was once thought honest & beloved;
but now his pardon is beg'd upon that acount—Tho he had
the honour at M[r] Bromleys Election,[204] when he came to vote
to have it loudly proclaim'd D[r] Shaw votes for M[r] Trevor,
which piece of Respect was paid to no one but himself. NB
The reason of this was a Misfortune the D[r] Labours under
not knowing his | own mind for one single Moment which   *fol. 32v '46'*
made them resolve that all the Convocation house shoud be
asured he was steady long enough to pronounce the name of
M[r] Trevor—that being <t>his Minute in the D[rs] thought—
three days in Xmas the<y> Sing a Song, in order to prepare

<hr>

[200] Joseph, who became an advocate of Doctors' Commons. They went on
to have Anne, who was twice married; and William, who died young: *ODNB*.

[201] See above, note 188 with *ODNB* article there cited. Shaw travelled widely
in the Islamic East making careful observations on all its physical and human
aspects, surviving robbery and kidnap in the process.

[202] He first travelled East in order to become chaplain to the English factory
at Algiers: *ODNB*.

[203] *Travels, or, Observations Relating to Several Parts of Barbary and the Levant* (2
vols., Oxford, 1738). It was well received at first but criticisms surfaced later
in Richard Pococke's *Description of the East* (2 vols., London, 1743–5) where
Shaw was attacked for inaccuracies, although the main controversy was over
the formation of the Delta. From Shepilinda's comment it appears that such
misgivings began to be felt from the outset.

[204] The reference is to the 9 Feb. 1737 by-election for an Oxford University
M.P. occasioned by the death of George Clarke, who has already appeared as
a donor of books and money to Worcester College (above, p. 4) and whose
donations to Queen's are about to be described here. The contestants were
William Bromley, son of the earlier M.P. with the same name (Tory) and Robert
Trevor, first Viscount Hampden (1706–83), fellow of All Souls, the only Whig
to contest an election in the first half of the eighteenth century. He lost, but
polled a respectable 27% of the vote. Bromley died almost immediately but
Trevor did not contest the 31 Mar. 1737 by-election. Shepilinda seems to be
saying that Shaw wanted to make a point of voting Whig but couldn't trust
himself to remember his candidate's name.

themselves for the ancient Ceremony of Singing up the Boar's head[205]—I wish their Voices are not clearer the 1st night than ye last, for I have heard that Mild ale is an Antidote to Singing—Good Dr Clark[206] whose Virtues as well as his charities are Inimitable gave many Gifts to this College; amongst the rest a very fine picture of Mary Queen of Scots, the sweetest I ever saw, drawn in a Lawn[207] habit, which Covers her[208]——

fol. 33r '47' Queens College is beholden for its Name <to> Philippa King Edwd the 2nds Wife; but the real Founder was her Confessor Robt Eglefield who in 1340 by her favour bought the Ground & built the Collegiate Hall—its Estate & number of Stipendaries were enlarged by the King & his Consort: the Society consists of a Provost 14 Fellows 7 exhibitioners 2 chaplains &C. It has been lately rebuilt with great Splendour ye sides being 372 feet long on one of them is the new Chapell & hall on the other a Magnificent Library full of Books ye Provost's & other Spacious Lodgings supported by piazzas & adorn'd with Statues the Visitor is the Abp of York

[PEMBROKE]

fol. 33v '48' Pembroke is the next College: Indeed I shou'd have spoke of it before ; but I forgot it ; so take it now. its a little place that stands in a By Corner, near unto peny-farthing Street:[209]

---

[205] The Boar's Head carol supposedly originates at Queen's and was sung with a feast of the Boar's Head on Christmas Day. This was continued until recent times and now takes place at a gaudy in early January. [MR]. For words, music, and photographs, see Taunt 1905.

[206] Dr. Clark is George Clarke, fellow of All Souls, who gave a great collection of his prints to Worcester College. He gave his own college six pictures of queens, of which one is mentioned here. [MR]

[207] 'A kind of fine linen, resembling cambric': OED.

[208] Lane Poole 1926, vol. 1, p. 113 (no. VI.15): 'gauze wings above each shoulder and veil; black dress with white satin quilted yoke'.

[209] Pennyfarthing Street is what is now known as Pembroke Street. [AI]. It was 'The street that commemorated the name of the great burgher-family, the Penyverthings, of whom one was Provost in Henry the Third's time': J. R. Green in Stainer 1901, p. 99.

the Chappell is new Built pretty & neat ; but I think too light for a Chappell[210]—There is nothing remarkable here except My Love Blew Breeches;[211] a pretty, Smart[212] Wight as ever peep'd under a Square Cap: with a Tuft ont;[213] the Master is D[r] Pantin[214] a Married Man with a family—poor Wretch he has the Gout, & a Palsie but I cannot help that, so good night to you Pembroke

Pembroke College so called in honour of the Earl of   *fol. 34r '49'*
Pembroke Chancellor of Oxford at the time of its being founded AD 1624 by Thomas Tisdale Esq[r] and Ric: Wight-wick BD before which time it was a nursery of learning Called Broad Gate Hall[215]—It has a Principal 11 Fellows 15 Scholarships &c The Quadrangle[216] is handsome in its front

[210] The Chapel was, indeed, new, being consecrated in 1732. By 'light' Shepilinda must mean the colour of the stone: the interior is rather gloomy. [AI/GN]

[211] 'Blew Breeches' or 'I'll love no more' was a popular dance tune from *c.* 1725. The melody appeared in John Walsh's Third Book of *The Compleat Country Dancing-Master* (London, 1735, p. 178), and then with the figures in the popular handbooks, e.g. posthumous editions of John Playford (1623–87; e.g. *Introduction to the skill of Musick* (15th edn., London, 1703)). It was an obvious nickname for a handsome young gentleman, particularly if he wore breeches of that colour on at least one occasion. [AI/GN]

[212] Not completely clear. 'Smart' seems to have been corrected from 'Smars' but the result might be intended to be 'Smarts'. No pun on surname 'Smart' or 'Wight' or 'White' seems to be supported by Foster, *Alumni*. 'Smart' meaning dandy referred to dress and might apply to noblemen or gentlemen commoners.

[213] Square cap with gold tassel ('tuft') marked a nobleman; with black tassel, a gentleman commoner; without tassel, a commoner; round cap without tassel, a servitor. See Midgley 1996, pp. 12–13, but note that the illustrations do not agree with the descriptions as far as tassels are concerned.

[214] The Master was the Revd. Matthew Panting (Master 1714–38), a rather enigmatic figure about whom there is next to nothing in the archive. [AI] Foster, *Alumni*: 'Panting, Matthew, s. M., of Oxford (city), pleb. Pembroke Coll., matric. 5 Nov. 1698, aged 15; B.A. 1702, fellow, M.A. 1705, B. and D.D. 1715, master of his college 1714–39, rector of St. Ebbes, Oxford 1714–19, vicar of Colne Rogers, co. Gloucester, 1718 until his death 12 Feb. 1738/9'.

[215] The foundation details are correct (Thomas Tesdale and Richard Wightwick being the founding benefactors, Tesdale posthumously) and the building that was originally Broadgates Hall is now part of the College site. [AI]

[216] There was only one quadrangle at the time. The gardens to the west into which the Chapel protruded eventually became Chapel Quad. [AI]

neat & Regular and the Garden is very pleasant. The Visitor
is the Chancellor of the University.——

[CHRIST CHURCH]

fol. 34v '50' Now pen do thy Best for Cristchurch is to be thy employment
This College was part of it Built by Cardinal Wolsey all indeed
except that Part of it called peckwater & the fine new Library,
which at present is only a fine Shell with a Beautifull venetian
Window at each end—gave by a D[r] Rattcliff[217] but they must
be longer lived than I that live to see it finish'd[218]—the Hall is
a very curious piece of Architecture being extremly large &
only Suported by one Single pillar[219] which is not at all heavy
& yet has strength Sufficient for its ofice—the Chappell is very
well the organ good M[r] Goodson[220] Organist—the Library is
a fine Room and well furnish'd many Books & Cuts gave to
it by the valuable & Worthy Dean Aldridge whose picture of
a 3 quarters size Drawn by S[r] Godfrey Kneller[221] adorns the
fol. 35r '51' over end of the | Library[222]—in the place where they lock up

217 Anthony Radcliffe was incorporated from Cambridge and elected to a
Studentship (Fellowship) by the Visitors in 1649. He was not removed after the
Restoration and was made a Canon and D.D. in 1681. His benefaction of £3000
to rebuild Peckwater Quad was received in 1706 but, once it had been decided
to build the 'finest' library across the south side, progress was slow and further
money had to be raised. At the time of Shepilinda's writing it was only a shell.
See Curthoys 2012, pp. 287ff.

218 It would not be finished until 1771 and, indeed, Shepilinda died before
1746.

219 Obviously the Hall stairs, not the Hall itself! The fan-vaulting was
commissioned probably by Samuel Fell in the 1640s and was built by a mason
with the helpful name of Mr Smith! [JC]

220 When she gets to the end of fol. 37r Shepilinda will forget that she has already
mentioned the organ and Richard Goodson and will write about them again (at
slightly greater length). Notes are attached to the reprise rather than here.

221 Lane Poole 1926, vol. 2, pp. 40ff. (no. XIII.98). Illustrated in Historical
portraits 1905 (pl. XIX, no. 211), Hiscock 1960 (frontispiece), and Curthoys 2012,
p. 139.

222 This probably refers to the Old Library, which remained in use until the
New Library in Peckwater Quad was finished. When Aldrich left his books a
new gallery was built to accommodate them. [JC]

their Rarities, is a small picture of him in Water Colours; the most lively Representation in Miniature I ever Saw[223]—There are many feasts[224] for the Opticks of the Curious here, but I forget them all except the Magick Lanthorn[225]—now I will shut the Library Door & Skip nimbly across the Quadrangle to Great Tom to tell you that the stairs by which you ascend are very Curious—they all wind round one post[226] & are allmost numberless—The Bell is large enough[227] to contain many people under it & some (but I don't know how many) may stand upon the Clapper Scrip & comp: went under it & stood upon the Clapper but I chose not it being too dangerous an experiment for my timerous nature[228]—There is a fountain in the Midle of the great quadrangle[229] but as it is neither the | largest nor the handsomest I ever saw I will leave it as I find it, for it signifies nothing to dwell too long upon so trifling a Subject, when—so many Material ones Call my Stubbed Goose Quill—there are some Statues over the

fol. 35v '52'

---

[223] Unlocated.

[224] Written over an erasure.

[225] This is certainly the second item listed in Thomas Wright's inventory of the scientific instruments left to Christ Church by Charles Boyle, 4th Earl Orrery, an inventory composed within a month of Boyle's death, viz. 'A MAGICK LANTHORN six figures'. When Robert Gunther examined the cupboard in Christ Church soon after the First World War the item was missing (Gunther 1923–67, vol. 1, p. 380) and so cannot be in the Museum of the History of Science, to which the Orrery Collection of instruments was moved in the 1930s (the College keeping the books) unless it came to light later on. [JC/GN]

[226] There is a spiral staircase which leads up to the bell in Tom Tower around a single newel post. [JC]. See the illustration in Butler 2006, p. 47.

[227] The bell Shepilinda saw was replaced. The present one measures seven feet one inch in diameter and five feet nine inches in height, and weighs six and a quarter tons. There is a photograph in Curthoys 2012, p. 134, but the scale is difficult to judge, which makes it unclear what was involved in standing on the clapper.

[228] It was not unusual until relatively recently for tourists to climb Tom Tower and even to ring the bell for a small charge. [JC]

[229] Mercury was dug in 1670 after part of the college burnt down, as a reservoir against future disasters. Originally the fountain was a globe but it was replaced by a statue of Mercury when the globe fell into disrepair. The first Mercury was pulled down in 1817 by Edward Geoffrey Smith Stanley (the future Earl of Derby and three times Prime Minister) while an undergraduate, and it was not replaced until the 1930s. [JC]

Gates but whether they are Kings Queens Archbishops or
Emperors I cant say[230] for I never observ'd them enough to
Say of what tribe they are—the Cannons all live in the great
Quadrangle they have all Lodgings or rather Houses—Some
of them are Married Some Widowers Some Batchelors or at
least reputed so—Dr Friend[231] has a Wife[232] a very Deserving
Woman as I readyly believe for <u>he</u> Scrip and <u>She</u> Scrip, both
say so, & they are oracles[233]—there is a handsome walk here
called the whites Walk,[234] it is long and well Gravell'd: but
Miss Gardener[235] (who is a very pretty Woman) & I don't like
it half so well as St Johns Grove

now I have nothing more to say, of this Coll: but of
(Mr Battley's[236] Favourite) the Dean;[237] and I wont say all
I know of him for it would be call'd Scandal if I spoke

---

[230] Queen Anne is over Tom Gate on the inside but it is almost certain that
the niche outside remained empty until Wolsey was put there in the 1880s.
[JC] Hearne noted (13 Aug. 1717): 'Going this day through X^t Church, I took
the opportunity to view distinctly the Statue just put up in one of the nitches
within the College, by the Dean's Lodgings, of B^p Fell. The Statuary was at
work': *Hearne*, vol. 6 (OHS xliii), 80. [GN]

[231] Probably Robert Freind (1667–1751), Student 1686, Censor 1700, and
Canon 1737: *ODNB*. [JC]

[232] He married Jane de L'Angle in 1713 and was survived by her.

[233] See Introduction, p. xx.

[234] The Broad Walk, which began life as the White Walk because of the
colour of the path. [JC]

[235] See the note on the poem 'How the St Johns men love Miss G-n-r'
(below, p. 73).

[236] Oliver Battely 1697–1762, whom Shepilinda 'cannot abide' a few lines
further on, appears in Foster, *Alumni* as son of Nicholas, of Canterbury (city),
cler., Christ Church, matric 8 June 1716, aged 19; B.A. 1720, M.A. 9 Mar.
1723/4, B.D. 1734, Proctor 1731, in which year he gave the Bodleian oration. He
married in 1741 and became Rector of Iron Acton, Glos. In 1745 he completed
posthumous publication of his uncle John Battely's *Antiquitates Rutupinae*.

[237] John Conybeare (1692–1755), matric. Exeter Coll. (he was from Devon)
1708, fellow 1710, B.D. 1728, D.D. 1730, Rector of Exeter 1730–3, Dean of
Christ Church 1733–55, Bishop of Bristol 1750–5. Married Jemima Juckes
(1703–47) in 1733 and had five children. He was a staunch Whig and was decisive
rather than diplomatic. His controversy in print with Richard Newton over the
latter's pursuit of a charter for Hart Hall was bitter and personal, and the year
before Shepilinda's *Memoir* he was leading the Whig opposition to the Tories
led by Newton: *ODNB*.

<u>Truth</u>—| he keeps a Wife, & a Taylors[238] Daughter: & has *fol. 36r '53'*
lately for his honesty Turn'd out one Mr Lamprey from
being Chaplain, because he wou'd not lend him his <u>Con-
science</u> to go to the election with: the Dean not careing
to appear in so publick a place without one—upon this
occassion^sic Mr Lamprey is gone to London and I hope
will come of with aplause when the <u>Most Worthy</u> Dean
found what he had done was not aproved even by his own
Party he Cringingly begg'd Mr Lamprey to accept of it
again & forget all animosities—but I know who would
be in the wrong to do so (Since I wrote this I hear poor
Mr Lamprey[239] is unjustly routed & the Dean holds up his
lumberly? head higher then ever I cant abide him nor M^r
Battley[240] neither) The Kitchen is a Noble Room & a great
Many Commons drest in it every Day the poor Students
of this | College are much oprest by the Dean and Can- *fol. 36v '54'*
nons & are allow'd nothing but Small Beer Mr Mead[241]

---

[238] Corrected from 'Talors'. Shepilinda is offended by the Dean's double
standards, and rightly so in respect of the mistress, but marriage was allowed
to the Head of this as well as many other Colleges.

[239] Thomas Lamprey had been a chaplain since 1714 but was turned out for
being married, which must have come as a bit of a shock as he had never made any
secret of his marriage and was completely unaware that chaplains were not allowed
to marry! In the end, it was decided that the chaplains had to resign their position
on marriage in the same way as the Students did. Lamprey was vicar of St. Mary
Magdalen, and later rector of St. Martin and St. Paul in Canterbury. [JC]

[240] The only indications of the unpleasantness which repelled Shepilinda are
Hearne's account of Battely's opposing, without good evidence, the conferring
of a doctorate on William Fullerton: (13 Apr. 1728) *Hearne*, vol. 10 (OHS lxvii),
5 and his alliance with the electors (including Robert Shippen of Brasenose and
George Huddesford of Trinity), who brutally overthrew the appointment of
John Andrews to Keepership of the Ashmolean in 1732: (22 Feb. 1732) *Hearne*,
vol. 11 (OHS lxxii), 31. For the latter, see also the lively account by D. J.
Womersley in his proctorial demission oration: *Oxford University Gazette*, 31
Mar. 2002.

[241] Richard Mead matriculated as a gentleman commoner in 1736. He was
possibly from Ireland, but we know virtually nothing else. [JC] Foster, *Alumni*
has: Mead, Richard, s. Richard, of London, doctor. Christ Church, matric. 10
July, 1736, aged 18; created M.A. 28 June 1739. (Revd. Mr. Mead, many years
secretary to the late bishop of Lincoln and Salisbury, died 22 Sep. 1766). [Foster's
parenthetical addition seems to be speculative.]

is a Gentleman Commoner here. there's an honour; for
Oxford cant boast of Such another—in this College there
was once a very learned Man[242] who had a great passion
for a Cat (I mean a 4 legg'd one) & made it his Study
night & day to have all manner of Conveniences for Lady
Puss—but the greatest difficulty was, how she might go
in & out of the Room when she had a Mind without the
Door being open'd & at last by the help of an able Joyner
he had a hole cut in his door for her Four legg'd Lady-
ship to use at her pleasure ; & he thought himself at the
height of Hapiness—when <u>oh! Direfull Catastrophe</u> this
same Cat was pleas'd To Kitten & put her Master to his
trumps what to do with all the little Misses ; & in a great
Consternation he went to one of his Fellow Collegiates
& told the dismall tale that he had Made a Door for great
puss to go in & out at But which way must‾the young
<ones> come—this Man being Something wiser than the
other | after a great deal of consideration Said he fancy'd if
the experiment were try'd that their little ladyships might
without any great Dificulty Travell through the Same
door their Mother did; but advised him to take care they
did not take <the> place of their Honour<a>ble Catship,
by coming before her into the room; this advice given,
the Cats Mother return'd him a thousands thanks, bow'd
profoundly, retired & found it answer in every respect;

fol. 37r '55'

---

[242] That Shepilinda does not know his name is unusual and in contrast to
the preceding Mr Battely narrative. It suggests we may be sceptical about the
story. Indeed, closer investigation shows that it has probably migrated from
Cambridge and was originally used to demonstrate how a savant may lack
common sense. John Wright, writing in 1827 of his time at Trinity College,
Cambridge, from 1815 on tells a handed down story of Isaac Newton (d. 1727)
having kept a cat which produced a kitten, whereupon he ordered the college
carpenter to make *two* holes of appropriate sizes in the door, not realizing,
despite his great intellect, that only the larger was required. Shepilinda retails an
Oxford version with a nameless protagonist, which makes the problem one of
etiquette that can be solved by training the kittens to yield precedence. Wright
supports his story by the 'evidence' that the door still had two visible holes,
albeit plugged: see Wright 1827, vol. 1, pp. 17ff.

there are many of this Kind in College now—but these
Sort of headpieces being so much in fashion there now (as
every one Strives to Copy the Dean) they are not taken
notice of—the organ is good here Mr Richard Goodson[243]
is organist poor Man he is much cumber'd with fat M^r
Will: Bertie[244] belong'd here more wit? then? ten? folks has
he there now he is a Cannonicall person——

Crist Church College was founded by Cardinal Wolsey in *fol. 37v '56'*
1525 & after his Disgrace carried on by K: Henry ye 8th and
Since then the Buildings have been Several times encreas'd
so they take up a vast extent of ground; they are August
& Splendid rather to be admired then exprest ; they have 2
Quadrangles, a lofty Cathedral; a Spacious Hall & Library;
noble walks, Gardens, Offices, &C: & an Hospital for 24
poor[245] the Foundation is of all others the most noble &
ample. It has a Dean 8 Cannon 101 Students 8 Singing men
8 Quiristers & a Master to Teach them Musick; an organist
School-Master, Usher, 40 Grammar Scholars &C: The
King is Visitor its length is 382 feet

[MAGDALEN]

Now to old Magdelene or Mawdling. I am arrived, better *fol. 38r '57'*
late than never. don't you agree with me in that, tho' I have

---

[243] Already mentioned on p. 48 above. This is Richard Goodson junior,
Professor of Music from 1718. Both father (*c*. 1655–1718), and son (1688–1741)
were well-known as musicians and performers. They both held the post of
organist at Christ Church. See *ODNB* article on Goodson, Richard (*c*. 1655–
1718), which also includes the son; also the introduction to the music catalogue
on the college website, http://library.chch.ox.ac.uk/music. [JC/GN]

[244] Foster, *Alumni*: Bertie, William, s. James, of Stanwell, Middx., arm.
Christ Church, matric. 18 June 1723, aged 17; B.A. 1727, M.A. 18 Mar. 1729/30,
B.D. 6 Mar. 1741/2, D.D. 1752, rector of Albury, Oxon. Parentage etc. in
Welch 1852, p. 285. For his membership of the Music Club, see Margaret Crum,
Bodleian Library Record 9/2 (1974), 98.

[245] The almshouse is now the lodgings of the Master of Pembroke College.
It was part of Wolsey's foundation and continued as such until the 1880s when
it was finally emptied and sold. We still have almsmen, usually long-serving
college servants, who are given a few pounds each year. [JC]

but little to say, & it won't tire my pen to say all I know
of this College—it has a Venerable look the Building low,
& bad enough, indeed the New Building[246] would be very
Handsome & (as M[r] Leigh[247] says) Magnificent did not the
Smallness of the arch you look through to the Grove[248] So
very much (Saving your presence) resemble a Glisterpipe[249]
(I must beg pardon for using so unsavoury a Simily) the
Grove is a pretty place the Deer in it[250] like the fellows very
fat ; the Bowling Green is very Comodious for Bowling
& drinking, the 2 Chief Studies of this Worthy Body. The
Water walk is very pretty, but little Frequented by reason
it is so near the Water There is a fine Alter piece in the
fol. 38v '58'   Chappell | the Organ loft is very Comodious the organ
I like but other folk's ears are so nice they dont Like it;
Truly I think more nice then Wise: pardon the proverb, for
Sancho panca was my great Uncle, & left me his proverbs
of a Legacy—the President is one D[r] Buttler,[251] who at this
time represents the University in room of M[r] Bromley[252]

[246] Built in 1733, five years before the *Memoir*.

[247] Unidentified. (Not the Master of Balliol mentioned on p. 9, who was Dr. Leigh.)

[248] In the centre of the New Building.

[249] Properly, clyster-pipe, a tube or pipe for administering clysters, i.e. enemas. Shapes vary but a diminishing cross-section is probably the feature which Shepilinda is seizing on to express her dissatisfaction at looking or passing through (from S.W. to N.E.) a small archway and then through an even smaller one. Both are indeed small given the scale of the New Building, although the overall effect is generally considered very successful. I am grateful to Hilary Pattison of Magdalen College Library for a valuable discussion *in situ*.

[250] von Uffenbach in 1710: 'There are numerous white and other stags and deer amongst which two, white spotted with brown, were as beautiful and tame creatures as I ever saw' (von Uffenbach 1928, p. 39). President Warren noted that 'There is an entry in the accounts of 1706 of £4 2s. for killing the does in the Grove, and the same again in 1707' (Warren 1907, p. 94).

[251] Edward Butler was President in 1738. He came up to Magdalen as a Demy in 1702, aged 16; was then elected a Fellow in 1710, and became President in 1722, a post he held until his death in 1745. He was Vice-Chancellor 1728–32, and M.P. for Oxford University 1737 until his death. He was a layman, which was very unusual for Magdalen Presidents. He was also a fund-raising genius, who got the money together to construct the New Building. [RD-S]

[252] William Bromley (1663–1732). Matric. from Christ Church 1679, B.A.

Diceas'd—a large big-boned Man—he was Vice=Can at
the Time that Dr Wilks was in love with me[253]—now for
College Customs upon May Day at 4 a Clock in the Morning all the Singing Men & Choiristers go to the top of the
Tower, & sing an anthem;[254] & the Quadrangle Is all drest
with Boughs & flowers and a Sermon preached[255] there at
10 a Clock in the Morning, in a Stone pulpit—theres one
Custom—now for another—one day in the year they call
the end of all things,[256] & this day the Burser delivers up
his accounts; & invites what company he has a Mind to
into the Bursery; the rest of the Coll: Sit in the Common
room & Send each a copy of verses to the Burser who is
Obliged for every copy to send them a quantity of Wine
| So they write & drink till Morning—I fancy they are   *fol. 39r '59'*
none of them Sober—I have one Custom more but I cant
put it down yet, so ex<c>use our Bess a little while. they
have many Comemoration days But I cant tell them—one
day in the year the Burser pays ever<y> fondationer from
Fellows to the Quiristers so much Money in the Chappell,
the demys have a groat apiece of silver the Quirister silver 2
penses, & the rest accordingly; I told you one thing wrong

1681, D.C.L. 1702, M.P. for Warwick 1690–8 and for the University 1701–32;
Speaker of the House of Commons 1710–13. See above, p. 45, n. 204, for the
by-election of Feb. 1737 contested by his son, also William.

[253] We do not know more of what happened with Dr. Wilks between
1728 and 1732 when Elizabeth was between 15 and 19 years old and the family
probably still living in Great Rollright. No Wilks/Wilkes of the right period
in Oxford and having either a Doctoral degree or membership of the medical
profession has been identified.

[254] See the article by Roy Judge referred to in note 62 of the Introduction.
The anthem was written by Thomas Smith, orientalist and scholar: Stanier 1901,
p. 120.

[255] Actually this is on a different day. Shepilinda will correct herself a little
further on.

[256] The account of the Bursar at Magdalen distributing wine for verses is
very interesting. We have read often of a custom at Magdalen from this time
called 'The End of All Things', which was some kind of party which took place
at the end of the financial year, but none of us knew what took place then! Now
we know. [RD-S]

& that is there is only an anthem sung on May Morning for the Sermon is preach'd upon Midsumer day; however I was right in the Circumstance tho' not in the Day; there are a small sprinkling of Gentlemen Comoners here. Tidy children enough when they're asleep;[257] Sr Lister Holt[258] Stalks loftily about this College, & thinks him self so very Considerable that no one else regards him: I fancy thats a Common Case, for where people seek respect, they often meet disgust.

fol. 39v '60'   Magdalen College was erected in 1458 by Wm Wainfleet Bp of Winchester its conveniences of all kinds are Such & the Endowments So large that it may Justly be accounted one of The most noble Foundations in Christendom Its buildings s{c}ituations & the delights of the Walks & groves adjacent thereto make it very note'd it has 40 Fellows a Schoolmaster 30 demys an Usher 3 publick Readers 4 Chaplains 8 Clerks 16 Quiristers an organist &c: the Bp of Winchester is Visitor its length is 297 feet.

[HART HALL][259]

fol. 40r '61'   Hart Hall is the first Hall I Shall tell you of it is a pretty little place enough my pappa was bred up a Gentleman Commoner here[260] the Principal is one Dr Newton,[261] who

---

[257] But no doubt rowdy when awake. Shepilinda then moves on to the arrogance which could be the corresponding vice of a nobleman.

[258] Sir Lister Holte was the son of Sir Clobery Holte of Aston, Warw., baronet, matric. from Magdalen 4 Feb. 1736/7, aged 15. He too became a baronet; he was created D.C.L. on 3 Apr. 1749, was M.P. for Lichfield 1741–7, and died on 21 Apr. 1776. [RD-S]

[259] Chartered as Hertford College in 1740.

[260] See Introduction, pp. xiii, xiv.

[261] Dr. Richard Newton (1676–1753). Foster, *Alumni* has: Newton, Richard, s. Thos., of Northampton (town), gent. Christ Church, matric. 16 June 1694, aged 18, student 1694, B.A. 1698, M.A. 1701, B.D. 18 Mar. 1707/8; D.D. from Hart Hall 1710, and Principal 1710–40, founder and 1st Principal of Hertford College 1740–52, canon of Christ Church 1752, rector of Sudborough, Northants., 1704–48, rector and patron of Lavendon, Bucks.; born at Yardley

is remarkable for writing 2 Books; one upon University Education,[262] & the other a most learned & labour'd dissertation upon Aple pye & Dumpling[263] 2 very material things

so they are, if you knew all that went to the making of 'em—but every one can't get them[264]

I believe[265] there is a Chappell here & Sometimes prayers when the principal has nothing else to do——

NB Hart Hall was converted into an Academical Nursery in 1314

Park 8 Nov. 1676, and died 21 Apr. 1752, buried in the chancel of Lavendon church. Dr. Newton was a controversial figure who was appointed Principal of Hart Hall in 1710 and thereafter dedicated his time and money to establishing it as a college. He was opposed by powerful interests, especially those of All Souls and Exeter (who had unclear rights to the land), and he did not shrink from arguing every controversy in print and in detail.

[262] Newton 1726. The book discusses the rules governing migration from one college to another, and was occasioned by one of his students, William Seaman, seceding to Oriel and another, Joseph Somaster, to Balliol, both in 1723. Newton argued that the fixed forty shillings fine levied on a college receiving a student who had not been officially released from his current one was not enough to discourage a reprehensible practice. See Hamilton 1903, p. 50.

[263] Newton did not actually write a book about apple pie and dumplings, but wrote about the subsistence costs of education as they affected both college and student (Newton 1733); and he published the proposed statutes for Hart Hall (Newton 1720). These works prescribed rigid micromanagement of matters such as provisioning. When it became known that the typical communal meal in Hart Hall was frugal, and might be apple dumplings, the way was open for *Terrae-Filius* to ridicule Newton's educationist pretensions and to adduce a new justification for a student seeking transfer to another college: 'Then as to diet, he [i.e. a head of college] may be full as oppressive again in that particular; ... he may ... confine me to a regimen of bread and water; or what is little better, of small beer and apple-dumplings', with the footnote 'Enjoin'd in a certain hall in Oxford, every Friday' (Amhurst 1726, Appendix, 'A letter to the Reverend Dr Newton', p. 305; Rivers 2004, p. 380).

[264] Added above the lines in another style or another hand.

[265] Hart Hall was apparently not on Shepilinda's visiting list, whether despite, or as a result of, the paternal connection cannot be known.

[ALBAN HALL]

fol. 40v '62' As to Alban Hall[266] I can't say much for the nobleness of its <u>Structure</u>—tho' the Principle D[r] Laban[267] has done his endeavours to make it as habitable as he can it stands pretty near Mertons Backside—The present principle is one D[r] Laban as yet not Married tho' Most people Conjecture he soon will for report says he is lustily promised to Miss Town a dainty fine Curious Young Lady[268]—(this match was Made by the Glorious D[r] Shippin)[269] This Gentleman now Stands for the Arabick profesors place & says when he has possession of the place he will endeavour to learn the Language[270] but I think it rather to[o] late for he is not

---

[266] St. Alban Hall became the property of its neighbour Merton in 1549 but was not incorporated into it until 1881, at which time there were 18 students. Physically it was a quadrangle of which the north range was rebuilt in 1599. Much was demolished 1905–10 and the rebuilt structure now forms St. Alban's Quad: Bott 1993, pp. 39ff.

[267] Shepilinda gives us what she had heard but not seen written. In reality this is Robert Leyborne (born 1693 or 1694) and we may infer that the second syllable was pronounced with an indefinite vowel. Foster, *Alumni*: Leyborn, Robert, s. Ant., of London, gent. Brasenose Coll., matric. 9 Mar. 1710/11, aged 17 (student of Christ Church 1712); B.A 19 Jan. 1714/15, fellow, M.A. 1717, Proctor 1723, B. & D.D. 1731; Principal of St. Alban Hall 1736–59, and rector of St. Dunstan, Stepney, 1729, and of St. Anne, Limehouse, 1730 until his death at Bath 13 May 1759.

[268] The chronological facts are so much at variance with what Shepilinda reports that she was clearly lied to. At this time Robert Leyborne had been widowed and was already remarried. He married Mary Feilding on 15 Aug. 1720 and she died on 12 Dec. 1731. He married Rebecca Town (born 4 June 1698) on 30 Jan. 1733, i.e. five years before the date of the *Memoirs*, and was married to her until her death on 18 Feb. 1756. The Principal's office did not require the holder to be unmarried (Robert's predecessor had been the son of the previous holder). If there was any reason for him to pretend to be unmarried then one is at a loss to explain the fact that it was public knowledge that he was about to marry Miss Town. It is also a puzzle to guess where and in what character she lodged. See Appendix D for the fulsome and, to modern ears perhaps, complacent memorial tributes Robert Leyborne composed for each of his wives.

[269] Robert and William Shippen (see above, Brasenose section, pp. 19–20) were Robert Leyborne's uncles. Westminster School records have: Leyborne, Robert, son of Anthony Leyborne, by Anne, sister of William Shippen ... QS (aged 15) 1708. (Barker & Stenning, 1928, p. 577.)

[270] The Laudian Professorship of Arabic had just become vacant with the

young tho' he is not married there is now no Inhabitants here except himself & Sister but once it was so full that they drest half a neck of Mutton in one day; nay Some authers go so far as to say it was all drest for one Diner—Alban Hall became an Academical Nursery in 1236

[EDMUND HALL]

Edmund Hall is the most ruinous place in Oxford all but *fol. 41r '63'* the Chapell which is very tight & pretty for not being Made any use of these some years it is little the worse for wearing Dr Felton[271] being afraid of taking Cold—I never heard of any body's belonging to this Hall since they were So cross as to expell Mr Winders;[272] from this place you have a Nice View of New College Bowling Green. NB they call Dr Felton Black Muzzle & blew beard, Indeed he is not handsome.

Edmund Hall purchas'd by Queens College for the purposes of Learning in 1557[273]

death in Jan. 1738 of John Wallis (appointed 1703). Leyborne's proposition may have been a sarcastic reference to Wallis having been an absentee professor who, since 1728, had entrusted all teaching to the Lord Almoner's Professor of Arabic, John Gagnier, who was appointed in 1717 to give instruction in the absence of the Laudian Professor. See *ODNB* article on Gagnier.

[271] Foster, *Alumni*: Felton, John, s. Henry, of St. Sepulchre, London, doctor. St. Edmund Hall, matric. 14 May 1730, aged 18. (His younger brother William was no longer at Edmund Hall in 1738.)

[272] Foster, *Alumni*: Winder, Thomas, s. John, of Preston, Lancs., gent. Brasenose Coll., matric. 29 Apr. 1726, aged 19; B.A. from St. Edmund Hall 1730, vicar of Cockerham, Lancs., 1737. Hearne wrote to him in Jan. 1735 hoping he would provide information on Lancashire antiquities, but he observes 'he was a very civil, pretty, comely Gentleman, but wanted to be taken care of by his Tutor and others that were to inspect him. But they were remiss': (24 Jan. 1734/5) *Hearne*, vol. 11 (OHS lxxii), 415. *VCH* notes: 'Ultimately he became deranged, and Cockerham was under sequestration for many years before his death' (*VCH Lancs.* viii. 92, n. 49). He died in his living in 1781.

[273] This was the year in which Ralph Rudde died. He had defied William Denysson, Provost of Queens and holder of the freehold in his own name, when he moved to the Hall and paid the rent punctually. Only when he died was Denysson able to transfer the freehold to the College (Kelly 1989, pp. 28–9).

[NEW INN HALL]

fol. 41v '64' New Inn Hall[274] is a Mighty Neat place tho' not fine The principle is the Ingenious D[r] Tovey[275] a Man so learned that he has wrote a Book; but it is a Secret to me what it is;[276] he being of a calm sedate Temper is Generally Moderater in the disputations in the Schools; he is remarkable for his fine Tast & polite Table; & is the very pink of Courtesy in all his behaviour—a very fit Companion for the ceremonious M[rs] Cockma[n][277]

New Inn Hall was given to New {Inn}[278] College Anno 1392[279]

Thereafter the exact relationship between College and Hall was often unclear. It was in 1903 that Magrath, the modern discoverer of Shepilinda, attempted as Provost of Queen$ to take over the Hall completely but was defeated by the Principal, Edward Moore. After the debate in Congregation, the *Oxford Magazine* noted that 'Oxford opinion has now come round to the view that the extinction of small Societies is not in itself desirable' (Kelly 1989, pp. 98–102).

[274] After being deserted in the Civil War New Inn Hall was once more an academic hall in name but in fact had no students and a principalship which had become a sinecure. It was assimilated into Balliol in 1887 and the surviving part eventually became Hannington Hall, the dining hall of St Peter's College.

[275] D'blossiers (or Bloshier) Tovey, matric. 1709, D.C.L. 1721, clergyman 1723–32, returned to Oxford in 1732 to take up the post of Principal of New Inn Hall.

[276] He had already published a pamphlet: *The Winchester converts* ... (Oxford, 1735), but Shepilinda has heard of the new and important work published in the year in which she writes, without knowing its title or subject. It was *Anglia Judaica: or the history and antiquities of the Jews in England* (Oxford, 1738). The *ODNB* article, 'Tovey, D'blossiers [Bloshier] (1692–1745)', notes that this 'has remained a major source for the history of the Jewish community in Britain', but warns that the Revd. S. Levy in his 1907 Presidential address to the Jewish Historical Society of England had observed that 'He made long and frequent quotations from the works of his two predecessors, Prynne and Madox, but he fell a victim to the perverse habit of forgetting the use of inverted commas. Eventually he became so absent-minded that he thought entirely original what he had simply copied or borrowed from other sources.' Levy goes on to note that this plagiarising had already been attacked by P. C. Webb in 1753. See 'Anglo-Jewish historiography', *Transactions of the Jewish Historical Society of England*, vol. 6 (1911), 9.

[277] Referring back to above, p. 26 and note.

[278] Shepilinda has inadvertently repeated the word.

[279] 'In 1391 the Bishop granted two messuages called Trilleckynnes [i.e.

[MAGDALEN HALL]

Magdalene Hall a hanger on of the College of that name[280] *fol. 42r '65'* a Strange Antiquated place looks like a tater'd Remnant of Ruin; fit only for the Nightly Visitations of Ghosts & Goblins the Principal is Dr Cotes[281] proffessor of Rhethorick[282] who being a lover of Dismall Dwellings, chose this, & the House M[rs] Levings[283] lived in upon the Gravell Walk for his habitation. I supose the Man is of a Gloomy Constitution, & loves damps & darkness. he has a Wife & children many

Magdalene Hall belongs to Magdalene College & was founded in 1480———

Trillecks Inn] with three gardens adjoining, and one messuage called Rose Hall with one garden adjoining to the Warden and Scholars of New College' (Mallett 1924, vol. 2, p. 301). For details and conjectural reconstruction, see Pantin 1964, pp. 71–9.

[280] It was the grammar school of Magdalen College situated in what is now its Longwall Quad. It became an academic hall in the sixteenth century. When it was badly damaged by fire in 1820 it moved premises to a building on the corner of Catte Street and New College Lane, which represented the abortive first founding of Hertford College. In 1874 it became part of the refounded Hertford. The remaining portion of the original School is now the old Grammar Hall in Magdalen's St. John's Quad (Hibbert 1988, s.n.). Shepilinda's description suggests that the Hall had become very run down in the early eighteenth century.

[281] Foster, *Alumni*: Cotes, Digby, s. Charles, of Coleshill, co. Warwick, gent. Magdalen Hall, matric. 31 May, 1698, aged 14; fellow All Souls' Coll. & B.A. 1707, M.A. 1711, Public Orator 1712–46; Principal Magdalen Hall 1716–45, rector of Hempstead, co. Gloucester, 1715, vicar of Coleshill, co. Warwick, 1716, canon of Lichfield 1734 until his death 11 Jan. 1745.

[282] No such chair existed but the title is sometimes used to refer to the office of Public Orator.

[283] Probably widow of Baptista Levinz, matric, from Magdalen Hall 1660, Fellow of Magdalen College 1664–83, d. 1692/3. She was the daughter of James Hyde (1618–81), Principal of Magdalen Hall 1662–81 (Brockliss 2008, p. 247). The house was clearly uninhabited since her death (at an undetermined date).

[ST. MARY HALL]

fol. 42v '66'   Sᵗ Mary Hall²⁸⁴ the Principal is one Dʳ King²⁸⁵, a very Clever man, & very fit to govern {:} So many Young Scholars as are under his care—the Hall it self is not fine but the Dʳˢ Lodgings are not only fine, but quite Elegant, large & Convenient & most Genteely furnish'd; in his Study is a very fine picture of Homer done by a most Celebrated hand; Mʳ Hart²⁸⁶ the poet is Tutor here, & is very Sollicitous about the Welfare of his Pupils; he has a great Many, so 'tis to be hoped some of them will come to good; the principals garden is Small, & nothing extra[or]dinary in it except some aple trees in pots; & great plenty of Kitchen Stuff (for they love good eating here)

Sᵗ Marys Hall was granted to Oriel College in 1325——

²⁸⁴ A building on the corner of High Street and Oriel Street was originally the rectory of St. Mary the Virgin and housed an academic hall whose scholars founded Oriel College in 1324 and shortly after moved to the adjacent Oriel site. In 1327 the hall became St. Mary Hall and continued until 1902, having been flagged for extinction by the 1877 Commission. Oriel's St. Mary's Quad includes portions of the original Hall, while its Rhodes Building is partly on the site of the original rectory: Hibbert 1988, s.n., *VCH Oxon*. iii. 129–31, and (for its early structure) Pantin 1964, pp. 41–4.

²⁸⁵ Foster, *Alumni*: King, William, s. Peregrine, of Stepney, Middx., cler. Balliol Coll., matric. 9 July 1701, aged 16; B.C.L. 1709, D.C.L. 1715; bar.-at-law, Gray's Inn, 1712, an advocate of Doctors' Commons 20 Jan. 1716, secretary to Duke of Ormond (Chancellor of the university), Principal of St. Mary Hall 1719 until his death 30 Dec. 1763. He became the leader of the Jacobite faction and was famous for his speech in the Sheldonian on the occasion of the opening of the Radcliffe Camera in 1749; the message of his successive clauses beginning 'Redeat' was scarcely ambiguous and drew loud applause: *Bodleian Quarterly Record* 1/6 (1915), 170 and Godley 1908, pp. 257–9.

²⁸⁶ Foster, *Alumni*: Harte, Walter, s. Walter, of Chipping Norton, Oxon., cler. St. Mary Hall, matric. 22 July 1724, aged 15; B.A. 1728, M.A. 21 Jan. 1730–1. As an undergraduate he was introduced to Alexander Pope and there was a degree of mutual encouragement and co-operation thereafter. His *Poems on several occasions* was published in 1727, a verse *Essay on satire* in 1731, and an *Essay on Reason*, in which he was assisted by Pope, in 1735. As Shepilinda notes he attained great reputation as a tutor at St. Mary Hall and in 1740 was elected vice-principal. Between 1746 and 1750 he was travelling tutor to Philip Stanhope, the addressee of *Lord Chesterfield's letters to his son*. He died in 1774: *ODNB*.

['FROG HALL']

Frog Hall:[287] The Principal is William Sheppard Esqr. This *fol. 43r '67'*
is but a small Building, and never a regular Front: the
Principal has a Wife & one Daughter (that's me) & a great
Fat Dog—there are no Curiositys here nor any particular
Customs, except one, which is that the principal will not
let any Member of his hall Sleep untill the Morning[288]—for
by long Study he has observ'd that too much Sleep is very
prejudicial not only to the health, but that <it> is apt to dull
the Understanding, & people's Geniuses now want rather
whets than repellers[289]———
This Hall was revived November 29 1736[290] but I say it's the
oldest Foundation in Town

[THE BODLEIAN]

The Bodleian Library *fol. 43v '68'*
Sr Thomas Bodley having in view the future state & pres-
ervation of this library, at his own Charge raised a gallery
all round the Quadrangle over the publick Schools to the
Intent it be furnish'd wth Book[s] when the other part was
filld—this Library has since been encreas'd by thousands of

---

[287] Oxford boasted many Halls with unromantic animal names (Ape Hall,
Worme Hall, etc.) but no Frog Hall appears to be documented. It is no surprise,
of course, that Shepilinda indulges in a comic renaming of the family dwelling,
here and in the poem on p. 69, but it has the unfortunate consequence that it
cannot be located. The only information we have is the comment on p. 10
(Balliol): 'The Masters Lodgings are Bad, (& Inconvenient) only one fine large
Room (which by the way my Mamma often longs for).'

[288] This sounds like the *cri de coeur* of a daughter whose father will not let
her lie in of a morning.

[289] If these are her father's actual words then Elizabeth's wit and delight in
wordplay may well originate in the liveliness of Sheppard family conversation.

[290] Probably a humorous reference to the date the Sheppards moved in. It
may not have been their first Oxford residence.

Books[291] he dyed Jan[ry] 1612[292]

[HORNBLOWING ON MAY DAY]

fol. 44r '69' in the City of Oxford there is a custom on May Day for all the Boys in town to blow horns which that they may be perfect in they begin to blow from the first of April but of the particular Morning they begin by 2 a Clock[293] The Tradition of this is that once upon a time the Tradesmen of this City went all out a Gathering May in a morning

---

[291] 'As for the public Library in Oxon ... his Will was that upon a foresight he had that in process of time there would be great want of conveyance and stowage for Books, ... then over the tops of those two stories, ... there should be contrived another third room ... for by that means there would be gained a very large supplement for stowage of books when the other Libraries should be fully replenished': Wood, *Hist. Univ.* ii (2), 789. See Craster 1952, pp. 9–13, especially 'it was not brought into general use for book-storage until 1824' (p. 11); see also Philip 1948, pp. 23ff.

[292] i.e. 1613 (new style).

[293] All night long, according to John Aubrey: 'Memorandum: [the night before the first day of May] at Oxford the Boyes doe blow Cowshorns and hollow Canes all night': Aubrey 1972, p. 136. Hearne, noting that horns were used as cups from ancient times, has this: ''Tis no wonder, therefore, that upon *the jollities on the first of May* formerly, the custom of *blowing with*, and drinking in, *horns* so much prevailed, which, though it be now generally disus'd, yet the custom of blowing them *prevails at this season, even to this day, at Oxford ...*': Hearne 1724, Preface, p. xviii; quoted in Brand 1849, vol. 1, p. 212). Circa 1848 John Richard Green and his fellow Magdalen College Schoolboys on 1 May 'used to ... gather in the grey of dawn on top of the College tower ... There was a long hush of waiting just before five and then the first bright point of sunlight gleamed out over the horizon; below, at the base of the tower, a mist of discordant noises from the tin horns of the town boys greeted its appearance, and above in the stillness, rose the soft pathetic air of the hymn *Te Deum Patrem colimus*' (Stainer 1901, Introduction, p. iii). Beatrice Batty describes the complete drowning out of the May Day anthem by between twenty and fifty boys with cowhorns on Magdalen Bridge when the 1882 widening was still incomplete (Batty 1888, pp. 2–3) and again in 1883 (ibid. 21). In 1907 T. H. Warren, President of Magdalen, mentions 'the blowing, still kept up, of the May horns by the populace' (Warren 1907, p. 106), but by this time they had begun to accept that they should cease blowing for the duration of the anthem itself (Bloxham 2002, p. 76, quoting the *Oxford Times* of 8 May 1909: it was only 'as the music [of the hymn] died to silence [that] the discordant music of the May-horns rose from the street').

in which time their Wives made them all *Cuckolds*[294] So to
warn all honest Mechanical Husbands to keep from May
Frolicks & take care of their spouses at home[295] this has been
the plague of my life these 2 months allmost

[ST SCHOLASTICA'S DAY PENANCE][296]

another custom there is that the Citizens don't like—once
upon a time the Schollers had a strong fancy to a Trades-
mans daughter & siezed upon the lass in a place they call
Logick lane. The townsmen being much Exasperated rose
in a Body & made a | Brave Resistance against the gown &   *fol. 44v '70'*
to make short of my Tale kill'd three score For which Insult
the Mayor & his Brother Aldermen are obliged every 10th of
January or Feb[ry] I can't tell which to go to St Maries Church
with hempen Cords about their Necks & pay as many silver
penys as the slain The<y> now follow the old Custom

[294] Word largely erased. The cuckolding allegation is otherwise only found
in *Companion* 1762, p. 8: 'Some pretend that this antient and notorious usage at
Oxford of blowing horns on May-day, typifies the genial season of cuckolding.'
Since the horns were blown or drunk from and do not decorate heads the idea
is seriously strained.

[295] The only *reason* given for the hornblowing in other sources is quite
different: 'It was also the custom at Oxford a generation ago for little boys to
blow horns about the streets early on May-day, which they did for the purpose
of 'calling up the old maids' ... 'Calling up the old maids' no doubt refers to
the practice of calling up the maids, whether old or young, to go a-maying'
(Thiselton-Dyer 1900, p. 260).

[296] It is not clear whether it is Shepilinda or her informant who has confused
a student rape case with the Swyndelstock Tavern incident as the trigger for the
St. Scholastica's day riot of 1355, in penance for which the Mayor, Bailiffs and
sixty burgesses had to go bareheaded (*not* in halters) to a memorial service every
10 February and each offer up a coin in memory of the University victims to
the total of 63 pence. A footnote in the Life of Anthony à Wood reads: 'The
traditional story that the Mayor was obliged to attend with an Halter round
his Neck, which was afterwards, to lessen the Disgrace, changed into a silken
String, has no real Foundation' (Anonymous 1772, vol. 2, pp. 296ff.), and Ayliffe
attributes the story to '*Londinensis* ... with whom I cannot agree' (Ayliffe 1723,
p. 133). The ritual of the memorial service and the pence was not scrapped until
1826, and in principle Shepilinda could have witnessed it, but it is clear from her
account she did not.

in every resp[ect] but one & that is the<y> wear a Silken
Rope instead of a Hempen one but if you will Tak[e] my
Opinion a Rope is a Rope let it be in what Shape it will &
I wish they all (may) deserve better)[297] xxxx[298]

[297] The unbalanced parenthesis is original.

[298] The three or four characters, possibly signature initials, remain
undeciphered.

THE POEMS

The 2nd part & End
of Sheppy
for Scrip
Containing
Poems
odd lines
Fragments
& Small
Scraps
May 2nd
1738

each one did admire

that ever the Squire
   Should dote on so ugly a fury
Many miles would I trudge
Cou'd I be but her Judge
for I'd hang her without any Jury.[1]

———

a somewhat in shape of a ballad[2]

God prosper long from being lost
   the people of frog hall[3]
but oh! I fear that to their Cost
   a Woe shall them befall

[1]   With this amusing jingle to open her personal anthology we seem to find Shepilinda on the verge of inventing the limerick, but it is probably the end of a longer poem now incomplete through loss of one or more leaves, especially as the first line is crowded against the top of the page and there is no title. This was the view of P. S. Spokes in his catalogue entry: 'followed (fol. 45) by a collection, incomplete at the beginning, of topical verse' (Spokes 1964, p. 75).

[2]   In this poem Shepilinda's facility in rhymed verse reinforces the humour of the melodramatic scene- setting which introduces her complaint about a romantic setback and her scolding of Cupid.

[3]   See above, p. 64.

portents & prodigies appeard
    that terrified their sight
the darkness of the Night was Cleared
    the Hemisphere shone bright
the Clouds were blazon'd all wth Red
    the Stars no lustre gave
with Argent darts the sky was spread

    A Scene disarm'd the Brave

but now this wondrous things disclos'd
    & Fully Made appear
a Damsell is to Love disposd
    which passion is severe
A poison old has gain'd her heart
    A Story Strange to tell
Sure Cupid shot his sharpest dart
    Indeed it was not well
long time in Oxford did she rove
    before her heart was won
but now she is all over love
    & spends her time alone
Thou Nasty Paltry Sneaking Youth
    why didst thou use her so
Thou doats't on lies & hatest truth
    leave'st hearts sincere in Woe

fol. 46v '20'

To Wound her lover quickly hast
    that Mutual be their flame
That all love may never Waste
    Nor Rivals break the Chain

———

Now you shall hear how the
St Johns men[4] love Miss G—n—r[5]

The poet having made the Sun shine the air
    Clear
I'll try to move in a Poeticall Sphere
Tho' a Vulgor one 'tis—I needs must confess
but who were the actors I'll leave you to Guess
Theres allways one Phoenix on Earth to be found
& She in St Giles's[6] lives hard by the pound[7]
he<r> person so sweet so Melodious her tongue
She has kill'd at St Johns both the old and y^e
    Young
She has late been so ill wth the heart palpitation
that St Johns Men to Cure her deal much in
    purgation

---

[4]   Identification of the six names reduced to consonantal skeletons in lines 13 and 14 is greatly facilitated by the availability of Sillery 1990. They are fellows of St. John's in their late twenties to mid-thirties. Shepilinda correctly titles the two who already have their doctoral degree in 1738. Two of the six are destined for eventual Presidency of the college.

[5]   This is Miss Gardener 'who is a very pretty Woman' (above, p. 51), accompanying Shepilinda in Christ Church Meadow; who is 'the Beautious good humour'd & gay' (below, p. 83), visited during a Saturday walk with Scrippy; and who is described in the final couplet of the last poem in the collection as the centre of attention at the concert (below, p. 90). She is certainly Grace Gardiner (1716–77), only surviving child of Bernard Gardiner (1668–1726), Warden of All Souls 1702–26 and Vice-Chancellor 1712–15, and related to the Roche Court branch of the Brocas family. Grace, named after her mother (daughter of Sir Sebastian Smith), was to marry Robert Whalley M.D. (1714–69) originally of Clerk Hill, Lancs., then of Tackley, Oxon., on 29 July 1742 and have six sons and two daughters. See Burrows 1886, pp. 239–40 with pedigree chart at end, and Burke 1841, p. 213. I am grateful to Margaret Williamson who searched the register of births for me.

[6]   In 1772 the former house on the site of no. 14 St. Giles was occupied by Mrs Whalley (Salter 1912, p. 53). Note that no. 18 was occupied by 'Mrs Gardiner': this could not have been Grace's mother who died in 1747 but may have been a relation. Both houses are on the east side of St. Giles, although Grace seems to have grown up in a house on the west side (see below).

[7]   'In St. Giles, north of the St. Mary Magdalen church, was a group of houses called Middle Row, closer to the east side than the west, and north of it the pound': Salter 1926, pp. 255ff.

believing that Sympathy has such a power
that Still[7] at the purge She Must Mend ev'ry
    hour
M^r S—th[8] M^r D—r<——>m[9] & M—g—e[10] the
    Tall
D^{rs} W—k—r[11] & B—k[12] M^r G—n[13] had a Call
all physick'd away in hopes to appease
this Phoenix's illness and give her some ease
beside 20 More that I allmost forget
who blooded and purg'd & each night took a
    Sweat
this voilent disipline they *underwent*
has left in their Rooms an *Unsavoury Scent*[14]
But as long as they've cured her no longer they
    Mou[rn]
their wits are Improved by't no more they're
    forlorn

---

8   Thomas Smyth, matric. 1722 (aged 15), Fellow (Founder's kin) 1722–42.

9   William Derham, matric. 1721 (aged 18), Fellow 1721–48, President 1748–57. See p. 7 (a charming man, possessor of many rarities) and p. 8 (owner of the finest cat in the college).

10   Either James Musgrave, matric. 1727 (aged 17), Fellow (Founder's kin 1727–9; Law 1729–47), Vice-President 1744; or Thomas Musgrave, matric. 1735 (aged 18), Fellow (Founder's kin) 1735 until his death in 1755. 'The Tall' must be an epithet used to distinguish one brother from the other.

11   William Walker, son of an Oxford city physician, matric. 1719 (aged 15), Fellow (Founder's kin) from 1719, D.C.L. 1736. Principal of New Inn Hall 1745–61. Elected President of St. John's in 1757 but resigned after a few months because of poor health. He died in 1761.

12   William Buck, matric. 1717 (aged 14), Fellow from 1717, D.C.L. 1736, held a succession of college offices and was twice Vice-President.

13   Richard Green, matric. 1726 (aged 18), Fellow (Merchant Taylors') 1726–56, B.D. 1739, D.D. 1743.

14   Partially erased.

To a person that was pleased to say I was in love[15]

Miss Betty what are you in love
hey-day why in that sphere d'ye Move
Love is a Joke & Sure you know it
—Oh:—it was that made you turn poet
now prithee tell me who's the Swain
that did your heart so strangely gain
is he a God or a Musician[16]
no—harkee—'tis a young Physician
is't of the body or the Mind
I fancy of the latter kind
a parson[17] Surely thats enough
to fill my head with bombast stuff
of Tithes Chickens Geese & Calves
& Some times take their tithes by halves
No! Give me a lover Blythe & Gay
that with Sweet Trifles Spends the day
with teazing Wit does me provoke
& without Censure lets me joke
Talks not in politicks but Rhymes
& panejericks drops by Times
praises my person and my Air
'tis such a youth must me ensnare
But why d'ye think I'm Such a fool
To love & make Myself a Tool
to every trifling Silly Ass
No—I'm another kind of lass
So far 'tis true I love—my Ease
& all the World I fain w^d please

---

[15] The title defines the situation and the poem starts lightly enough but then turns into a quite savage and lengthy tirade against marriage. Shepilinda was clearly very annoyed by the incident, and the last line may suggest she wrote the verses the same evening.

[16] Written over erased 'Magician'.

[17] If Elizabeth failed to marry a College Head then she might well be expected to settle for a Fellow taking up the next vacant living.

But thats a trick I ne'er Cou'd learn
& others faults I won't discern

for Scandal is a crime I hate
& every thing that brings Debate
So never tell me I'm in love
for that's a thing you cannot prove
So don't presume friend any more
to lay your baby's at my door
& father every brat on me
believe me S^r that shall not be
for truly I'm above your Scandal
& surely will not hold the Candle
to light your fire & be your Screen
No—that will me too much demean
I never lov'd nor ever Will
so let each Jack provide his Gill
if you still say I am in love
out of this place you ne'er shall move
your very Words you shall devour
& Scarcely shall survive one hour
was it in earnest or in play
that you these words of late did Say
pray let me know for I'm a poet
& in your downfall soon will shew it
No—love I hate, abhorr, despise,
Such Trumpery Stuff Compos'd of lies
Madam I die's—a pretty word
Such language sure 'tis most absurd
this is the Wit of every lover
& all that I cou'd e'er discover

a whining lovers but an Ass
& a Silly oafish lass
that listens to their Idle Tale
& lets those empty Words prevail
they all will tell you that they die
Unless you're kind but they all lie

believe them not—but think like me
& then two Fools will ne'er agree
Some tell us that an Ancient Maid
is the Worst thing that can Invade
but I deny it flat & plain
'tis a State wish'd for oft in Vain
there's nothing in a Married life
but feuds & Jaws & Scorn & Strife
Pray[18] Think what every Woman feels
With Children draggling at her heels
In raggs & tatters all be patcht
Not only Married but they're matcht
he daily to the Tavern goes
She stays at home to mend his Cloath\<s\>
This is a Marriage Scene display'd
& should be known to every Maid
Now—when I have such bliss in View
how can \<you\> think I'll e'er love true
Good night'ye S^r I'll scratch no more
but leave you in your den to roar
for envy Bitterness & Spight
that I have cleared myself to Night

a pretty love pastoral I made it Tho'[19]

Ye verdant shades & cool refreshing groves
Secure retreat & friend to all the loves
let me enjoy thy Zephyr Blowing Shade
& not to flattering Fops be e'er betray'd
thy Fragrant Breezes Calm a Troubled Breast
& on thy Grassy surface let me rest

---

18 Written over erasure.
19 A very competent exercise in the pastoral genre, with Sidney (mistakenly designated Pembroke), referred to as the model. It may have the same origin as the previous composition (note 'I did resolve no More to Vex / but ever to abhorr the faithless Sex') but it has the calm of its artificial setting.

The Voilet<s> & Daizey's spread the ground
& all the flowery Sweets do here abound
the Water Curling? Down in purling rills
descending from the Steep & Craggy hills
the little Sheep & wanton heifers play
& in the Meadows Innocently Stray
the Nymphs & Swains are wholly Unadorn'd
politeness & fine dress by them are scorn'd
this is the View of the Arcadian plains
that Pembroke lofty poet so explains
2 Shepherdesses lately thither Stray'd
one Antiquated——'tother a young Maid
who sitting under a green spreading Tree
Disclosed their thoughts which did not well
  agree
Melintha (Young) the first that Silence broke
& to the aged Doris thus she Spoke
Oh! dearest Doris pri'thee tell me when
thou first tookst an aversion to the Men
what was the Cause——now be sincere and tell
was not there many Swains that loved thee
  well
or was it only one false hearted Swain
that in Your Youthful days your heart did
  gain

fol. 49r '25' then left thee for Some other Lowlier Maid
& thy Soft head by flattery betray'd

DORIS: Melintha Fair I'll tell the real truth
in former days there was a Blooming youth
his Name was Linco Beautious Was his Face[20]
& the Most Wealthy Shepherd on the place?
he danced with me at ev'ry rural Ball
which Made Me envied by the Maidens all

---

20 Written over erasure.

three Happy Months I thought my self Secure
but flames so fierce as his cou'd not endure—
I well remmember 'twas the first of May.
A Yeoman's Daughter hither beat her way
She danc'd & drest & Sung wth so much art
She Gain'd my Linco's double meaning heart
I ne'er Mistrusted I had lost my Swain
till one day Tripping o'er the verdant plain
to gain an hour in this Same Calm retreat
Here did I see young Linco at her feet
Breathing those Vows, which once to me he
    made
'twas then—I found I surely was betray'd
'twas then I did resolve no More to Vex
but ever to abhorr the faithless Sex
Now Since to you I have confessed the Truth
pray let me know what Sprightly looking
    Youth
of all your Number does the fairest Stand
to tie in Hymens hall the Marriage band
is it young Coridon of Beautious Mold   *fol. 49v '26'*
or does your heart delight in Clito's Gold
Come let thy little heart be once Sincere
& tell me who's the Swain you prize most
    dear

MELINTHA: Doris you raise Such blushes in my face
    that all my former paleness does displace
    not Coridon nor Clito's lov'd by me
    & yet I Can't Sincerely Say I'm free
    the Gay Melampas Sues me for his Bride
    & 'tis to Him my trem'bling Heart I've tied
    But See—we are disturb'd—so must no more
    but shall your pleasing Company deplore

An odd sort of a thing that came into
my head in Gloucestershire[21]

Ye fair nymphs of Slaughter attend to my ditty
it neither pretends to be sprightly nor Witty
but 'tis to Amuse you I now try my Skill
& of laughing I trust you shall both[22] have y^r fill

it is of pease kids & beau blossoms I sing
the sweets of the field & the Joy of the Spring
2 Beaus with these titles Infested those parts
with a Cruel Intention to steal away hearts

Beau Blossom the youngest was airy & smart
but pease kid was hansome by Nature not art
he caused loves passion in Many a Maid
but let him take care that he is not betray'd[23]

fol. 5or '27'

From Iford[24] a Ramble to Bourton we took
& all the Gay folks of that garden forsook
to young Mr Jourdens[25] we then did repair
to breath the delights of the Horse chesnutt air

[21]   Clearly an account of an actual journey, and probably an actual encounter with an aged would-be suitor.

[22]   i.e the nymphs of both Upper and Lower Slaughter.

[23]   The transition that follows is very abrupt and raises the possibility that a leaf has been lost.

[24]   Eyford 'a small extra-parochial village in the hundred of Slaughter, Gloucester, 5 miles from Stow …; containing 11 houses and 57 inhabitants' (Capper 1808, s.n.).

[25]   John Jordan (1713–74); 'young' to distinguish him from his late father, also John (c. 1667–1732). He has a fine tomb in Bourton Churchyard. The family originated from Fulbrook.

From poppy's we went with our hearts very Glad
where we met M^{ss} Dorothy[26] on her Bay pad
like the sign of Queen Bess this fair damsell did
    ride
with baskets & ban-boxes tied to her side

Next morning to Breakfast she us did invite
which caus'd in our stomachs much Joy &
    Delight
to think we shou'd tast of Sr Richard Dubs[27] Cheer
For our Stomachs were good tho' his looks y^l
    were queer

To pleasure our palates, it was her Intent
So to India to ?Kuts? she a messenger sent[28]
Her Cakes toast & Butter were excellent good
which to Scrippy & I are most Heavenly food

W^d you think it—Sr Richard much wanted a wife
to make him Sack possets & nurse his old life
for which purpose he Trampt all the country
    round
but a wife to his purpose will never be found

---

[26] The most notable 'Miss Dorothy' living in or near Bourton-on-the-Water at this time was undoubtedly Dorothy Vernon (date of birth unknown, died unmarried 1764). By her will she would establish Dorothy Vernon's Charity for the future relief of the poor of Bourton, Lower Slaughter, and Clapton. In 1738 she was probably in her fifties or sixties. Her brother Charles, rector of Shadwell St. Paul, Middx., had died two years previously aged 57. The other brother Richard (1674–1752, so now 64) was still Rector of St. Lawrence's in Bourton in succession to his father, George Vernon (1638–1720). There is no record that Richard ever married and Dorothy may well have kept house for him at the Rectory (see next note).

[27] Not traced and probably a pseudonymous use of the name of Sir Richard Dobbs, a famous Lord Mayor of London in 1552. This may be Richard Vernon disguised by Shepilinda in order safely to satirise the old man's attempts to woo her.

[28] Reading uncertain and reference undetermined. Perhaps a quality grocer in Stow-on-the-Wold. ('Kuts' may just possibly represent *Coutts*).

Miss Dolly she tells him that a Marriage State
is often attended wth scorn & wth hate
& those terrible words of for better & worse
tho the[29] the young ones delight is old Batch-
    elors Curse

fol. 50v '28'

& If he should think of a gay airy Spouse
'tis a hundred to ten but she Blazons his *Hous*
gives him for his coat armour a large *pair of Horns*
& a *household* a Name all the Country *Scorns*

& now good S[r] Richard I bid you Adieu
but the thoughts of a wife—beg you w[d] not
    persue
But take the advice of your whimsicall Friend
which Brings my dull Ballad at last to an End

This was wrote on an old fool a lover of mine

Chaos a good Sort of a Creature
if you Mind it but you may Chuse
whether you will or no, I can do no better[30]

If Scrip c[d] Imagine how hard 'twas to write[31]
She ne'er wou'd ask Sheppy So much to Endite
however, once more I'll endeavour to please
    her
tho' I think such dumb Nonsense more likely
    to teaze her

---

[29] MS. has 'the the'.

[30] A cryptic three-line *jeu* unrelated to what comes before or after.

[31] An apologetic preface to the following narrative poem describing, at Scrippy's request and in a racy tempo, a round of visits made one Saturday.

the theme I forget so {so} am quite in the Dark
Stay—she Said I must Sing how we walk'd in
    the park[32]
On a Saturday Morning the Sun shining bright
To stretch our Supporters[33] & Gladden our
    sight

When all the Smart gownsmen to dinner[34] were
    gone
excepting Apollyon who thither had flown
to contemplate what mischief he w^d go about
what vice he'd encourage what virtus he'd rout

But we left there & soon found the way[35]
To miss gardener[36] the Beautious good
    humour'd & gay
To chat a few Moments, tho' we were in hast
for our dinner was ready—and we were not
    drest

_____

Our Victuals soon swallow'd we sallied again   *fol. 51r '29'*
To hear Mr Munday[37] perform a sweet Strain
whose wit & good Nature makes him appear
    gay
For tho' Dark is his Sight he'll most charm-
    ingly play

_____

[32] Florence Gamlen (1856–1952) recalls that in her early childhood, 'Of course we went for walks. Sometimes in the Parks, then a grass field with a cart track across it from East to West, approached from St. Giles by a footpath between hedges, where Keble Road now is' (Gamlen 1953, p. 14).
[33] legs.
[34] See above, p. 47, n. 212.
[35] Along the footpath mentioned above (note 32).
[36] See above, p. 73, n. 5.
[37] Unidentified.

When we left Mr Mundays we next took our
　　Station
In Merry King Alfreds Royal Foundation[38]
where we had a B^r a Civilized Youth[39]
Tho' his room it was Chaos to tell you the
　　truth

———

To pretend to describe it is labour in Vain
& To give their assisstance^sic my Muses wont
　　deign
So I think that they are an Unhavourly[40] Tribe
& my spirit's to<o> lofty to give them a bribe

———

For they say since the death of our Good
　　Caroline[41]
that ev'ry dumb poet has beg'd for a line
these petitions So numerous Makes them afraid
of having poor pegasus rode to a Jade

———

In the Room lay promiscuously Musick &
　　bread
Cards, Nightcaps, & bands, a great Needle &
　　thread
to stich up sometimes in his stocking a hole
a paper of pins a Small Sack of Sea Coal

———

[38] University College.
[39] See pp. 28–9 and Introduction, pp. xx, xxi.
[40] See p. 31, n. 125.
[41] See p. 4, n. 12.

his <u>Wife</u> in the Corner stood out of the Way[42]
Maps, Divinity, Logick lay litter'd like hay
with Candlesticks, Stean Pot[43] & Bason for
    hands
which were foul'd with Soap Suds—he'd been
    washing his Bands

———

as Scrip & I laugh'd to think we came so pat in
appear'd M[rs] Worcester wth Fresh frames of
    Matting
She look'd very Sower to think we came there
While her Master was gone to the Chappell to
    prayer

———

Said the Room it was never so Dirty before   *fol. 51v '30'*
& her Master w[d] ne'er let it be so no more
Then she talk'd Scrub'd the Room & made us a
    fire
tho' our Company's she Did not greatly desire

———

then we went to New College an Anthem to
    hear
But were much disapointed no Anthem was
    there
So soon to our B[rs] again we return'd
The Coffee was made & the fire it burnt

———

---

42 The line reads oddly, as if 'wife' is a humorous reference to something else (a portrait?). At the least it must indicate a very shy and withdrawn personality to take no part in the ensuing barbed exchange between the visitors and the housekeeper.

43 A two-handled clay vessel for liquids (later, solids as well).

M[r] Snow[44] he came in & an Anthem he play'd
the Finest that ever by Weldon[45] was made
that over we gave to our Visit an end
& Both took our leaves of our B[r] & friend

The Following wrote upon Somebody[46]

Since all my hopes like tinder are destroy'd
My griefs are With the Blackest Sable dyed
I cannot bear the pain that now I feel
but must my Secret thoughts to you reveal
our Friendship shall supply the place of Love
& rigorrous parents ne'er shal that remove
alone I will frequent this lonely plain
& all your Sex for ever will disdain
Sincere I allways was & ne'er knew art
enough to hide the Secrets of my heart

a limb of the Same horse[47]

To the worthiest & best of my Sisters I write
who I hope my poor offerrings[sic] with love will
          requite
For the worms in my head are begiñing to work
& Some whims in my Brains do Most Secretly
          lurk
No Satyr heroick nor Such Severe Stuff
For I think panigericks for Nimphs are enough

fol. 52r '31'   Not to trouble their hearts with the town nor y[e]
          State

---

[44] Perhaps John Snow, 'organist of St. John's College; privilegiatus 23 Apr.
1741': Foster, *Alumni*.

[45] John Weldon (1676–1736), composer of anthems, songs, and a few
instrumental pieces: *ODNB*.

[46] Apparently addressed by Shepilinda to a suitor vetoed by her parents.

[47] The first poem addressed to Scrippy after her long-term or permanent
departure.

for that must In{n}cur much displeasure & hate
then let all our songs be of Friendship so pure
that's more lasting than time will for ages endure
The noblest of passions we Mortals can find
that relieves our Sunk Spirits & Comforts the
    Mind
We often are troubled with many hard crosses
but a timely She friend soon repairs all our losses
Sometimes for a Fopish young fellow we're vex'd
then think we're in love & are sadly perplex'd
but I am too old to be catcht with those fancys
fit for nothing but Children & queens in
    Romancy's
I'm resolv'd to be merry & spend all my days
in thinking of you & rehearsing your praise
So I bid you adieu—& Adieu to my Lays

Upon our Rare Consort[48]

The Muses all to Visit me
are from parnassus Come
The<y> heard I was to write to thee
    which made them hither roam
to help me to endite sweet lays
& chaunt my friendly Scrippy's praise

2

Your letter gave me much delight
but that I need not tell
& In your absense pleas'd my Sight
    I won't express how well
I'm sure there's not so bright a Gem
Shines in the Royal diadem

---

48 The first half of this poem laments Scrippy's absence. The second gives
an account of the kind of music concert which is poorly documented before
Jackson's Oxford Journal began publication in 1753. See Burrows 1980, p. 177.

fol. 52v '32'

3

With joy I read it often o'er
with care perus'd each line
W^d Fate my Scrippy but restore
   & make her ever Mine
What Joy 'twould be to hear her Sing
& sweetly touch each Trembling String

4

My ink pots wept it self quite dry
   for grief that you are gone
My Goosequills all away did fly
   none left to write a Song
So crow quills of a Sable Hue
Tho' faint & weak must scratch to you

5

When Mr Fosset[49] Strikes[50] the Strings
   he does us all Inspire
but more when Mr Powel[51] Sings
   in Concert with his Lyre
Such Musick Sure Must charm our Ears
& quite dispell all Gloomy fears

[49] This is Richard Fawcett (1714–82) already encountered in the Corpus Christi section as 'a very pretty young Gentleman & plays finely upon ye Harpsicord' (above, p. 34, n. 139). He was a score copyist and employed others to copy scores as well. See Ward Jones & Burrows 2004, pp. 117ff.

[50] Written over erasure, probably 'Sounds'.

[51] Foster, *Alumni*: Powell, Walter, s. Martin, of Oxford (city), pleb. Magdalen Coll., matric. 17 Dec. 1714, aged 17; chorister 1704–14, clerk 1714–44, yeoman bedel of divinity; died 6 Nov. 1744; will at Oxford proved 3 July 1745. See Bloxam 1853, pp. 127–9. Hearne reports that he was 'a good natured man, & a good Singer, being Clarke of Magd. Coll. & singing man of St. John's': (26 Jan. 1732) in *Hearne*, vol. 11 (OHS lxxii), 21, and that he had sung at the concert given by Handel in the Sheldonian five years earlier 'as he hath done all along with them': (13 July 1733) ibid. 230. Noted by A. D. Godley (Godley 1908, p. 136). See Wollenberg 2001, p. 49 and p. 84 (obituary).

6

When Mr Hine[52] his heart's had eat
 he look'd about with Glee
then Tuned his Voil, took his Seat
 &?[?] was to play most free
The<n> quick to Him there did resort
Our Friend & favourite Davenport[53]

7

From Cristchurch next young Lewis[54] came *fol. 53r '33'*
the darling of each Fair
but who their passions e'er can blame
 His[55] beauty must ensnare
Such Musick from his Voil flows
that praises every one bestows

8

On Voiloncella as Bevil[56] play'd
 he did each hearer Charm
Apollo sure did give him aid
 & Moved his pliant arm
The Warbling of the linnetts throats
Were not so sweet as Bevils Notes

9

Tis true there was a Chatt'ring Swain
 with Bugles on his Coat
Who laugh'd & Show'd his teeth amain
 Nor listen'd to one Note

---

[52] No suitable Hine in Foster, *Alumni*.
[53] Unidentified. There are many of this surname in Foster, *Alumni* and several are possible candidates judging by matriculation dates.
[54] Unidentified.
[55] Written over erased 'Such'.
[56] Unidentified.

but eat & Consumd? & talk'd his *part*[57]
nor for the Musick Cared one *Fart*[58]

10

The Females was a beautious throng
　　all Scatter'd thro' the hall[59]
Most worthy of a poets Song
　　Brown Fair & Short & Tall
But sure Miss Gard'ner[60] gained the prize
on her was fixt each gownsmans eyes

folios 54 to 79 are blank

[57] Partly erased.

[58] Largely erased.

[59] 'As to the concerts we frequently have in our halls … If these were abolish'd, what a mortification would many of our smart fellow-commoners undergo, to be deprived of the pleasure of presenting tickets to the ladies, and ushering them into the hall': Smart 1750–1, vol. 1, p. 131. (Quoted by Midgely 1996, p. 141.) The words are those of a Cambridge correspondent but, writing to an Oxford journal, he clearly implies that they apply to both universities.

[60] See the notes to the poem about her, above, p. 73, n. 5.

DEDICATORY LETTER

Dedications are generaly at the Beginning of a Book which *fol. 80v*
made me chuse mine at the latter End[61]

Madam[62]
Your Surprizing worth & Boundless Generosity Embold-
ens me to take the liberty of dedicating this undeserving
Pamphlet to you, hoping when it has such a protector it
will Scape the Censure of the snarling Criticks—Since you
are pleas'd to cast a favourable Eye on some of the mean
productions of my uncultivated & Baren Genius which
yet has not nor ever can produce any thing worth your
acceptance, but if a Sincere heart & downright affections
will make an atonement for my great presumtion that you
may asure your self of But Madam with what Face can I
pretend to let my slight Scraps appear before so penetrating
a Judge, a person of your polite tast & Inimitable Acom-
plishments—& tho' your humility is so exceeding great
yet Madam, give me leave to say this—that the Sun in its
Meridian height shines not so bright as your Fair Self who
sparkle with a Brilliant Lustre over the rest of your Sex,
some of which in your absense pretend to display their
Frothy Eloquence but when you appear the Mist evaporates
& shows them to be Counterfiets, for their can be but one
Phœnix at a Time & that is yʳ bright self

The usual Stile of dedications is compos'd of Flattery which *fol. 81r*
agrees not with thy[63] old Fashion'd Temper—but would I
flatter how can I when the most sublime thoughts that ever

---

[61] A humorous exercise in exaggerated flattery consisting of compliments
with no actual content (and including ironic denigration of flattery).
[62] Although her name does not appear, this must be Scrippy.
[63] Written over erased 'My'.

flow'd from the most Elegant Quill must fall short of your
incomparable Merits—for what w^d be the Grosest Flattery
to others w^d be but a faint resemblance when set in Compe-
tition with your Fair Self who are so largely Endow'd wth
Invaluable Merits—and now Madam with begging your
acceptance of this as an additionall one to those Numbers
you have so often & so partially bestow'd on

Madam Your Most
Obsequious Vasall &
Obedient Humble
Servant to Command

   Altamira[64]

---

[64] Presumably 'Remarkably tall'. Scrippy seems to have been short: she
is addressed as 'little Scrippy' on p. 9; she 'sat down like a Fairy Queen in a
Cowslip' in the organ loft at New College (p. 39) and she 'stood upon the
clapper' of Great Tom (p. 49), which Sheppy declined to do.

LETTERS AT THE FRONT
OF THE MANUSCRIPT

Letter 1

Kirkstall Vicarage, Leeds Feb 5

Dear Dr Macgrath[1]——

The M.S.S you mentioned is at present in the hands of Mrs E.T. Turner (wife of the late Registrar)[2]—She has had it over 2 years I should think, and you are welcome to use it as you think fit. I fancy Mrs Turner said I should have it next time I called, but no one knows when that will be.

Yours sincerely
Neville Egerton Leigh[3]

---

[1] John Richard Magrath (1839–1930) was Provost of Queen's College, Oxford, 1878–1930 but became less active after 1911 when he lost his battle opposing the independence of St. Edmund Hall. He is the modern rediscoverer of Shepilinda (see above, Introduction).

[2] i.e. Mrs. E. S. Turner, wife of the *former* registrar in modern parlance (see note 4, below).

[3] Neville Egerton Leigh (1852–1929), Curate at Leeds Parish Church 1878–89, Vicar of Kirkstall 1889–1907, Vicar of Holy Trinity, Richmond, Yorks. 1907–26; bibliophile and collector. (Blackwells Catalogue No. 262, issued in 1929, was mainly devoted to Leigh's library, including his 'valuable Goldsmith and Thackeray collections, fine modern bindings, Kiplingiana, etc.'). Letter 1 is therefore to be dated before 1908 and most likely shortly precedes Letter 2 since that appears to be the response to a letter sent by Magrath, triggered by his receipt of Letter 1.

Letter 2

36 St Giles' Oxford Feb 9th 1903

Dear Mr. Provost

I herewith enclose M[r]. Egerton Leigh's M.S. and his letter to you concerning it: I have shewn the M.S. to several people here, none of whom have thought it worth printing in extenso—Thank you very much for your kind message to M[r]. Turner; & Expression about my health—I am thankful to say I am much better, but Influenza is not to be forgotten in a hurry!

Yours very truly

Emily S. Turner[4]

Letter 3

Broadwell Manor House, Moreton in Marsh February 28

Dear Dr. Warren[5]

Thank you very much for the loan of 'Sheppeelinda' which I now return. I wonder if it will ever be published. It is rather interesting. May I please have a postcard to announce its safe arrival. Again thanking you & apologising for all the trouble I have given.

Yours sincerely

Maude Egerton Leigh[6]

---

[4]   Emily Singleton Lightfoot married the Revd. Edward Tindal Turner, Registrar of the University of Oxford 1870–97, in 1875, from which time the couple lived in no. 36 St. Giles. Emily continued there after her husband's death in 1911 and remained there until 1916. She died the following year.

[5]   Thomas Herbert Warren (1853–1930), President of Magdalen 1885–1928, author of a short history of the college in 1907, which does not, however, mention or make use of the Shepilinda MS.

[6]   This is presumably (Laura) Maude Egerton Leigh née Edwards, Neville's sister-in-law, having married his brother Lieutenant Edward Egerton Leigh, b. 1854, in 1874.

Letter 4[7]

Queen's College, Oxford, 22 July, 1930

My dear Cowley,

I think I had better not delay forwarding to you for the presentation to the Bodleian of the enclosed MS. of which you have perhaps heard before. I have had it by me more than 25 years & in opposition to M[rs] Turner's opinion, think it will be well worth printing if it can be edited by a person who is willing by research to steep himself in Eighteenth Century Oxford Social life and to fit himself to explain and illustrate its somewhat libellous remarks.

I enclose some letters connected with it including one from its former owner who when he handed it over to me stated that he did not want it back and thought the Bodleian would be its proper eventual resting place. I had hoped before this to have had it edited & had so far succeeded that just before the war I had had it transcribed for the printer and handed it over to +. When the war broke out he was appointed to Portsmouth (I think[8]) but died[9] thus halting its progress. I with difficulty recovered the MS. but could not discover any traces of the transcript: Warren the old President of Magdalen[10] thought well of it.

Yours always
J R Magrath

+ I have forgotten his name. He was, I think a New College Man who was much interested in Eighteenth century Oxford especially I think in the Sport of those days. I think there are some notes or remains of his in Bodley.

---

[7] For discussion of this letter see above, Introduction.
[8] It was, in fact, Southampton.
[9] Of pneumonia contracted from guard-duty.
[10] See above, p. 94, n. 3.

Added in another hand (in pencil):[*]

This was P. Manning [Monogram] 24.vij.'30
The transcript was in the hands of Warland Andrew of
Bridge S$^{t.}$ Abingdon in 1930 [Monogram] 3.xj.1930

---

[*] The addition was initialled by Edgar Lobel of the Bodleian
Library, Dept. of Western Manuscripts.

WORCESTER COLLEGE
AND THE FATE OF BLACK BESS

*'the Laboratory where Black Bess (my Namesake) was Boiled, &
made into Soop'* (above, p. 3).

These thirteen words very near the beginning are the most
problematic, not to say disquieting, statement in the Memoirs.

The laboratory is undocumented.[1] *Black Bess* cannot refer
to Dick Turpin's mare because she had still not entered
the Highwayman's legend at the time of his execution
on 7 April 1739, over a year after the *Memoirs* were written, and there is no Oxford connection. She was not well
known before Harrison Ainsworth's *Rookwood* (1834) and
was largely, possibly entirely, his creation.[2] Nor is 'Black
Bess' known as a name for an unexceptional ingredient in
a recipe. In any case, a kitchen, not a laboratory, would be
more appropriate if that were meant.

In Oxford in 1738 the name, on present evidence, would
have to refer to an incident recorded by Thomas Hearne
nine years before:

---

[1]   Nothing is known of a laboratory at Worcester College or its predecessors.
[EG] The association may have come about because Sir Kenelm Digby was known
(a) to have attended Gloucester Hall and studied mathematics and astrology with
Thomas Allen and (b) to have had a laboratory. However, the laboratory was at
Gresham College at London and at a later stage in his life. [GN]

[2]   'The contemporary records, the newspaper reports, court archives and
official documents of the 1730s, are resoundingly silent about two of the key
elements in the modern construction of Turpin: there is no mention of the ride
to York, and no mention that Turpin ever owned a horse named Black Bess':
Sharpe 2004, pp. 137ff. Before *Rookwood* there is only Horace Smith's *Gaieties
and Gravities* (London, 1825) with a ballad 'Turpin & the Bishop' which begins
'Bold Turpin ... his black mare Bess bestrode': Sharpe 2004, pp. 154–60.

1729 Aug. 7 (Thur.) Yesterday was hanged at the Castle at Oxford, being condemned this last Assizes, a young Woman of about 25 or 26 years of age, commonly called Black Bess. She was a Shropshire woman by birth, but was never married, tho' she hath had several Children. She had been condemned several times before, but she was no sooner out of Jayle, but she used to return to her former Pranks, particularly horse-stealing, at wch she was remarkably famous, in so much that after Condemnation at the former Assizes at Oxford, having obtained a Pardon, that very afternoon she was freed, she stole two horses at Garsington, four miles from Oxford, and was taken the next day near St Alban's with a companion or two (but they were quitted), & being afterwards conveyed to Oxford was (as I have observed) hanged yesterday, making (as I am told) a penitent end.[3]

Hearne does not have anything to say about the disposal of Black Bess's corpse but it is very likely that it would have been taken by the university students for dissection by the University Lecturer in Anatomy or his Assistant.[4] Compare Hearne's account of the fate of Richard Fuller's body the following year:

1730. July 30 (Thur.). On Tuesday last (July 28) there was hanged at Oxford one Richard Fuller, of Caversham, in Oxfordshire, a young man of 26 years of age, for murdering his Wife. There was a sad work on that occasion, the Scholars endeavouring to get the dead body, assisted by some Townesmen, & others on the contrary hindering. The Relations had provided a Coffin to have it decently buried at Caversham, but the Scholars broke it all to pieces, the body being in it; after wch those opposite to the Scholars had it again, & so for several times sometimes one side had it & sometimes the other, but the Proctors, favouring the Relations, the body was at last delivered to them in order again for Caversham, & a second Coffin was made, wch the Scholars also broke, rescued the body, cutt off the Head, &c.; after wch 'twas again recovered for the Relations, and then got from them again & brought to

3   *Hearne*, vol. 10 (OHS lxvii), 164.
4   Frank Nicholls gave the anatomy classes about this time. (See Sinclair & Robb-Smith 1950, pp. 26ff.) It is not clear who conducted the demonstrations and dissecting but the archaeological investigations of the Old Ashmolean basement have shown that many took place there in the late seventeenth and early eighteenth centuries, even though they were curtailed when Bodleian readers objected to the smell: P. D. Mitchell *et al.*, *Journal of Anatomy* 219 (2011), 94a.

Queen's College, where 'twas made a Skeleton & the Flesh dispersed up and down.[5]

Black Bess the horse thief had no relations in Oxford to fight for her corpse and it must have gone for dissection, but this still leaves the macabre details of Shepilinda's phrases unexplained. The account would be less disturbing if she were simply referring to defleshing in order to produce a specimen skeleton, like the pair she saw in St. John's (above, p. 6), but her words make the 'soop'[6] not the skeleton the object of the exercise.

[5] *Hearne*, vol. 10 (OHS lxvii), 313. Another very similar story is recorded by Hearne: (Fri. 31 Mar. 1721) *Hearne*, vol. 7 (OHS xlviii), 228.

[6] *OED* has 'soop' as an eighteenth-century spelling of 'soup' but not of 'soap'. The present editor assumes that Shepilinda does *not* imply that the deliquescence was consumed, only that it had the consistency of soup. He will also welcome a convincing demonstration of an innocuous explanation of the passage.

SIR THOMAS WHITE'S LETTER TO THE FELLOWS OF ST. JOHN'S

Mr. President with the Fellowes and Schollers, I haue mee recommended unto you euen from the bottome of my hearte, desyringe the holye Ghoste maye bee amonge you untill the ende of the worlde, and desyringe Almightie God that euerye one of you maye loue one another as brethren; and I shall desire you all to apply your learninge and soe doinge God shall give you his blessinge both in this worlde and in the worlde to come. And further more, if any uariaunce or strife doe arise amonge you, I shall desyre you for God's loue to pacifye it as much as you maye; and that doinge I put noe doubt but God shall blesse euerye one of you. And this shall be the last letter that euer I shall sende unto you, and therefore I shall desyre euery one of you to take a copie of yt for my sake. Noe more to you at this time, but the Lord have you in his keeping untill th'ende of the Worlde. Written the 27th of Januarye 1566. I desyre you all to pray to God for mee that I maye ende my life with patience, and that he maye take mee to his mercye. By mee Sir Thomas White, Knight, 'Alderman of London, and Founder of St. John's Colledge in Oxforde. Obijt Anno Salutis, 1566 Regni Elizabethe 8[vo.] et die undecimo Februarii'[1]

---

[1]   C. M. Clode (ed.), *Memorials of the Guild of Merchant Taylors of the Fraternity of St. John the Baptist in the City of London* (London, 1875), pp. 692–712.

APPENDIX D

ROBERT LEYBORNE'S MEMORIAL
INSCRIPTIONS TO HIS WIVES

Robert Leyborne,[1] Principal of Alban Hall, produced notable memorial inscriptions on both occasions of his marital bereavement. There is a memorial tablet to his first wife, Mary, née Feilding, in St. Dunstan's and All Saints' Church in Stepney which reads:

> In Memory of / MARY LEYBORNE / Born Nov 1ˢᵗ, 1688 Deceased: Dec. 4ᵗʰ(?), 1731 / the Wife of / ROBERT LEYBORNE D.D. / Rector of this Parish / She was Pious, Cheerfull, Prudent, Liberal / in all the Accomplishments of Good Breeding / And Vertues of a Perfect Houswife / Most Excellent: / She wanted not Spirit, or Wit, / or a Just Knowledge of Her Selfe / Yet Her sole Ambition was to Please / Her Husband. / She had no Interest, or *Will* but *HIS* / Never was *Man* more *Belov'd,* / or *Woman Deserv'd* more Affection.[2]

When his second wife Rebecca, née Town, died in 1756 Robert buried her in the Abbey Church in Bath. Outdoing even his previous fulsome effort, he had the following monumental inscription carved:

> In memory of Rebecca Leyborne / Interr'd at the foot of this pillar. / Born *June* the 4th, 1698. / Deceased *February* 18th, 1756. / A wife more than twenty-three years to *Robert Leyborne*, D.D. / (Rector of the Churches of St. Dunstan Stepney / And of St. Anne's Middlesex near London; / And Principal of Alban Hall in Oxford,) / Who never once saw her ruffled with anger, / Or heard her utter even a peevish word; / Whether pain'd or injur'd, the same good woman,

[1]   See the section on Alban Hall (pp. 58–9) with notes.
[2]   For text and photograph by W. Foster and G. Gillon, see http://www.findagrave.com/memorial/ 70653997 (accessed 11 Feb. 2018).

/ In whose mouth as in whose character, / Was no contradiction: / Resign'd, gentle, courteous, affable; / Without Passion, though not without sense, / She took offence as little as she gave it; / She never was, or made an enemy; / To servants mild; to relations kind; / To the poor, a friend; to the stranger, hospitable; / Always caring how to please her husband, / Yet not less attentive to the one thing needful. / How few will be able to equal, / What all should endeavour to imitate.[3]

---

[3] Britton 1825, p. 117, who refers to 'a simplicity which may amuse our readers'; reprinted in Pettigrew 1857, p. 142.

BIBLIOGRAPHY

Ackermann 1814   R. Ackermann, *A History of the University of Oxford and its Colleges, Halls, and Public Buildings* (2 vols. London, 1814)

Adams 1996   R. H. Adams, *Memorial Inscriptions in St. John's College, Oxford* (Oxford, 1996)

Amhurst 1726   Nicholas Amhurst, *Terrae-Filius: or, The Secret History of the University of Oxford* (London, 1726)

Amhurst 1733   Nicholas Amhurst, *The Terrae-Filius's Speech, as it was to have been Spoken at the Publick Act, in the Theatre in Oxford* (London, 1733)

Anonymous 1739a   *A Faithful Narrative of the proceedings in a late affair between the Rev. Mr. John Swinton, and Mr. George Baker, both of Wadham College, Oxford ... sodomitical practices ...* (London, 1739)

Anonymous 1739b   *College-wit Sharpen'd: or, the head of a house, with, a sting in the tail ... Address'd to the two famous universities of S-d-m and G-m-rr-h* (London, 1739)

Anonymous 1772   *Lives of those Eminent Antiquaries John Leland, Thomas Hearne, and Anthony à Wood* (2 vols. Oxford, 1772)

Archer *et al.* 1988   M. Archer, Sarah Crewe, and P. Cormack, *English Heritage in Stained Glass: Oxford* (Oxford, c. 1988)

Aubrey 1972   John Aubrey, *Remaines of Gentilisme and Judaisme* in *Three Prose Works*, ed. J. Buchanan-Brown (Fontwell, 1972)

Ayliffe 1723   John Ayliffe, *Ancient and Present State of the University of Oxford* (2 vols. London, 1723)

Baker 1971   J. N. L. Baker, *Jesus College Oxford 1571–1971* (Oxford, 1971)

Barker & Stenning 1928   G. F. R. Barker and A. H. Stenning, *Record of Old Westminsters: A Biographical List* (2 vols. London, 1928)

Baskerville 1905   H. Baskerville, ed., *Thomas Baskerville's Account of Oxford*, in *Collectanea IV* (OHS xlvii, 1905), 175–225 [Partial edition of Bodl. MS. Rawlinson D. 810. Note that the contents page has 'written in 1683–6', which is to be preferred to '*c*. 1670–1700' in the chapter heading.]

Bate & Goodman 2014   J. Bate and Jessica Goodman, *Worcester, Portrait of an Oxford College* (London, 2014)

Batty 1888   *Some Oxford Customs*, by Bee Bee [Beatrice Batty] (London, 1888)

Bloxam 1853   J. R. Bloxam, *Register of ... Magdalen College in the University of Oxford*. [Vol. 1, *The Choristers*] (Oxford, 1853)

Bloxham 2002   Christine Bloxham, *May Day to Mummers. Folklore and Traditional Customs in Oxfordshire* (Charlbury, Oxon., 2002)

Bloxham 2005   Christine Bloxham, *Folklore of Oxfordshire* (Stroud, 2005)

Boase 1894   C. W. Boase, *Registrum Collegii Exoniensis* (OHS xxvii, 1894)

Bott 1964   A. Bott, *Monuments in Merton College Chapel* (Oxford, 1964)

Bott 1993   A. Bott, *Merton College, A Short History of the Buildings* (Oxford, 1993)

Brand 1849   John Brand (revised H. Ellis), *Observations on Popular Antiquities of Great Britain* (3 vols. London, 1849)

Brazen Nose	*The Brazen Nose: A College Magazine*, vol. 1– (Oxford, 1909–)
Britton 1825	John Britton, *History and Antiquities of Bath Abbey Church, including Biographical Anecdotes* (London, 1825)
Brodrick 1885	G. C. Brodrick, *Memorials of Merton College with Biographical Notices* (OHS iv, 1885)
Brockliss 2008	L. W. B. Brockliss (ed.), *Magdalen College, Oxford: A History* (Oxford, 2008)
Burke 1835	John Burke, *Genealogical and Heraldic History of the Commoners of Great Britain and Ireland* (London, 1835)
Burke 1841	John Burke and John Bernard Burke, *Genealogical and Heraldic History of the Extinct and Dormant Baronetcies of England, Ireland and Scotland* (2nd edn. London, 1841)
Burke 1863	Sir Bernard Burke, *Genealogical and Heraldic Dictionary of the Landed Gentry of Great Britain and Ireland, Part II* (4th edn. London, 1863)
Burrows 1874	Montagu Burrows, *Worthies of All Souls: Four Centuries of English History, illustrated from the College Archives* (London, 1874)
Burrows 1886	Montagu Burrows, *The Family of Brocas of Beaurepaire and Roche Court, Hereditary Masters of the Royal Buckhounds* (London, 1886)
Burrows 1980	D. Burrows, 'Sources for Oxford Handel performances in the first half of the Eighteenth Century', *Music & Letters*, vol. 61, no. 2 (April 1980), 177–85
Burrows & Ward Jones 2004	D. Burrows and P. Ward Jones, 'Musicians and music copyists in mid-Eighteenth-Century Oxford', in Wollenberg & McVeigh 2004
Butler 2006	C. Butler (ed.), *Christ Church, Oxford. A Portrait of the House* (London, 2006)

Buxton 1976   J. Buxton, *New College, Oxford. A Note on*
                       the Garden (Oxford, 1976) [16 unnumbered
                       pages]

Buxton & Williams   J. Buxton and P. Williams, *New College,*
    1979   *Oxford, 1379–1979* (Oxford, 1979)

Capper 1808   B. P. Capper, *Topographical Dictionary of*
                       the United Kingdom (London, 1808)

Catto 2013   J. Catto (ed.), *Oriel College. A History*
                       (Oxford, 2013)

Clifford 2004   Helen M. Clifford, *A Treasured Inheritance.*
                       600 years of Oxford College Silver (Oxford,
                       2004)

Colvin & Simmons   H. M. Colvin and J. S. G. Simmons,
    1989   *All Souls. An Oxford College and its Buildings*
                       [Chichele lectures, 1986] (Oxford, 1989)

Companion 1762   T. Warton, *A Companion to the Guide and*
                       a Guide to the Companion (London, 1762?)

Cordeaux & Merry   E. H. Cordeaux and D. H. Merry,
    1968   *Bibliography of Printed Works relating to the*
                       University of Oxford (Oxford, 1968)

Craster 1952   Sir Edmund Craster, *History of the Bodleian*
                       Library 1845–1945 (Oxford, 1952)

Craster 1971   Sir Edmund Craster, ed. E. F. Jacob, *History*
                       of All Souls College Library (London, 1971)

Curthoys 2012   Judith Curthoys, *The Cardinal's College*
                       (London, 2012)

Cymmrodorion   *Transactions of the Honourable Society of*
                       Cymmrodorion. [Sessions 1943–4] (London,
                       1946), [Sessions 1946–7] (London, 1948)

Dallaway 1815   J. Dallaway, *History of the Western Division*
                       of the County of Sussex (2 vols. London,
                       1815–32)

Daniel & Barker 1900   C. H. Daniel and W. R. Barker, *Worcester*
                       College (London, 1900)

Darwall-Smith 2008   R. H. Darwall-Smith, *History of University*
                       College, Oxford (Oxford, 2008)

Davies & Garnett 2009 — C. Davies and Jane Garnett (eds.), *Wadham College 1610–2010* (London, 2009)

Devereux & Griffiths 1976 — R. A. Devereux and D. N. Griffiths, *Worcester College, Oxford* (Oxford [? 1951], repr. with minor changes, 1976)

Drake 1699 — [James Drake], *The Antient and Modern Stages Survey'd* (London, 1699)

Emden 1948 — C. S. Emden, *Oriel Papers* (Oxford, 1948)

Evans & Richards 1983 — R. J. W. Evans and B. A. Richards, *Brasenose College: A Short Guide* (Oxford, 1983 [first published 1977])

Fasnacht 1954 — Ruth Fasnacht, *History of the City of Oxford* (Oxford, 1954)

Fenton 1811 — R. Fenton, *A Historical Tour through Pembrokeshire* (London, 1811)

Fiennes 1947 — C. Morris (ed.), *The Journeys of Celia Fiennes* (London, 1947)

Foster, *Alumni* — J. Foster, *Alumni Oxonienses: Members of the University of Oxford, 1500–1714* (4 vols. London, 1891); *Alumni Oxonienses _1715–1886* (4 vols. London, 1887) [Matriculation date determines which series is being referenced]

Fowler 1893 — T. Fowler, *History of Corpus Christi College with Lists of its Members* (OHS xxv, 1893)

Gamlen 1953 — Florence Mostyn Gamlen, *My Memoirs* (Oxford, 1953?)

Godley 1908 — A. D. Godley, *Oxford in the Eighteenth Century* (London, 1908)

Green 1979 — V. H. H. Green, *The Commonwealth of Lincoln College 1427–1977* (Oxford, 1979)

Green & Horden 2007 — S. J. D. Green and P. Horden (eds.), *All Souls under the Ancien Régime* (Oxford, 2007)

Guest 1991 — I. Guest, *Dr. John Radcliffe and his Trust* (London, 1991)

Guide 1827   *Oxford University and City Guide* (Oxford, 1827)

Gunther 1923–67   R. Gunther, *Early Science in Oxford* (15 vols., Oxford, 1923–67)

Hamilton 1903   S. G. Hamilton, *Hertford College* (London, 1903)

Hansen 1998   W. Hansen (ed.), *Anthology of Ancient Greek Popular Literature* (Bloomington, Indiana Univ. Press, 1998)

Heaney 2017   M. Heaney (ed.), *Percy Manning, the man who collected Oxfordshire* (Oxford, 2017)

Hearne   C. E. Doble *et al.* (eds.), *Remarks and Collections of Thomas Hearne* (11 vols. OHS ii, vii, etc. 1884–1918) [citations are prefixed with the diary date]

Hearne 1724   Thomas Hearne, *Robert of Gloucester's Chronicle* (2 vols. Oxford, 1724)

Henderson 1899   B. W. Henderson, *Merton College* (London, 1899)

Hibbert 1988   C. and E. Hibbert, *Encyclopaedia of Oxford* (London, 1988)

Hiscock 1960   W. G. Hiscock, *Henry Aldrich of Christ Church 1648–1710* (priv. print. Oxford, 1960)

Historical portraits   *Illustrated Catalogue of … Portraits of English*
    1905   *Historical Personages who died between 1625 and 1714* [Exhibited in the Examination Schools] (Oxford, 1905)

Hobbes 1849   J. R. Hobbes, *The Picture Collector's Manual* (2 vols. London, 1849)

Hobson 1954   M. G. Hobson (ed.), *Oxford Council Acts 1701–52* (Oxford, 1954)

Hone 1950   C. R. Hone, *The Life of Dr. John Radcliffe 1652–1714* (London, 1950)

Hopkins 2005   Clare Hopkins, *Trinity: 450 years of an Oxford College Community* (Oxford, 2005)

Hurst 1899   H. Hurst, *Oxford Topography* (OHS xxxix, 1899)

Jackson 1893   T. G. Jackson, *Wadham College, Oxford* (Oxford, 1893)

Johnson 1928   R. B. Johnson, *The Undergraduate* (London, 1928)

Jones 1987   F. Jones, *Historic Carmarthenshire Homes and their Families* (Carmarthen, 1987)

Jones 1997   J. Jones, *Balliol College: A History* (2nd edn. Oxford, 1997)

Kelly 1989   J. N. D. Kelly, *St. Edmund Hall: Almost Seven Hundred Years* (Oxford, 1989)

Kemp 2013   M. Kemp, *The Chapel of Trinity College, Oxford: 1691–94* (London, 2013)

Koenig 2013   C. Koenig, *Oxford Past Times* (Oxford, 2013)

Lane Poole 1912   Rachael Lane Poole, *Catalogue of Portraits*. Vol. 1. Portraits in the University Collections and in the Town and County Halls (OHS lvii, 1912)

Lane Poole 1926   Rachael Lane Poole, *Catalogue of Portraits*. Vol. 2. Portraits in the Colleges and Halls (2 parts, OHS lxxxi, lxxxii, 1926)

L'Estrange 1738   Sir Roger L'Estrange, *Fables of Aesop and Other Eminent Mythologists* (8th edn. London, 1738)

Loggan 1675   D. Loggan, *Oxonia Illustrata … nec non urbis totius scenographia* (Oxford 1675)

Magrath 1904   J. R. Magrath, *The Flemings in Oxford*. Vol. 1, 1650–80 (OHS xliv, 1904)

Magrath 1921   J. R. Magrath, *The Queen's College* (2 vols. Oxford, 1921)

Mallett 1924   C. E. Mallet, *History of the University of Oxford* (2 vols. London, 1924)

Marshall 1725   Marshall, *A Chronological Treatise upon the Seventy Weeks of Daniel* (London, 1725)

Marshall 1883

G. W. Marshall, *Miscellanea Marescalliana, Genealogical Notes on the Surname of Marshall* (2 vols. Exeter etc. 1883–8)

Martin & Highfield 1997

G. H. Martin and J. R. L. Highfield, *A History of Merton College, Oxford* (Oxford, 1997)

Mee 1911

J. H. Mee, *The Oldest Music Room in Europe* (London, 1911)

Midgley 1996

G. Midgley, *University Life in Eighteenth-Century Oxford* (New Haven and London, 1996)

Namier & Brooke 1985

L. B. Namier and J. Brooke (eds.), *History of Parliament: House of Commons 1754–90* (new edn. 3 vols. London, 1985)

Newton 1720

R. Newton, *A Scheme of Discipline with statutes intended to be established by a royal charter for the education of youth in Hart-Hall in the University of Oxford* (Oxford ?, 1720)

Newton 1726

R. Newton, *University Education: or an explication of the statute which ... prohibits the admission of scholars going from one society to another ...* (London, 1726)

Newton 1733

R. Newton, *The Expence of University Education Reduced* (London, 1733)

Nias 1918

J. B. Nias, *Dr. John Radcliffe: A Sketch of his Life with an Account of his Fellows and Foundations* (Oxford, 1918)

Oxoniensia

Oxoniensia, journal dealing with archaeology, history and architecture of Oxford and neighbourhood, vols. 1– (Oxford, 1936–)

Pantin 1964

W. A. Pantin, 'The halls and schools of medieval Oxford', in *Oxford Studies Presented to Daniel Callus* (OHS n.s. xvi, 1964)

Pattenden 1979

P. Pattenden, *Sundials at an Oxford College* (Oxford, 1979)

Pattenden 1980	P. Pattenden, *The Pelican Sundial: Description of the Tables* (Oxford, 1980)
Pemberton 1905	R. Pemberton, *Solihull and its Church* (Exeter, 1905)
Pettigrew 1857	T. J. Pettigrew, *Chronicles of the Tombs: A Select Collection of Epitaphs* (London, 1857)
Philip 1948	I. G. Philip, 'The building of the Schools Quadrangle', *Oxoniensia*, 13 (1948), 30–47
Playfair 1884	R. L. Playfair, *The Scourge of Christendom: Annals of British Relations with Algiers prior to the French Conquest* (London, 1884)
Pocket Companion 1756	*A Pocket Companion for Oxford* (new edn., Oxford, 1756).
Quiller Couch 1892	Lilian M. Quiller Couch, *Reminiscences of Oxford by Oxford Men, 1559–1850* (OHS xxii, 1892)
Rannie 1900	D. W. Rannie, *Oriel College* (London, 1900)
Ray 1737	J. Ray, *A Compleat Collection of English Proverbs* (3rd edn. London, 1737)
Richards & Shadwell 1926	G. C. Richards and C. L. Shadwell, *The Provosts and Fellows of Oriel College, Oxford* (Oxford, 1926)
Rivers 2004	W. E. Rivers (ed.), *Terrae-Filius, or, The Secret History of the University of Oxford* [by Nicholas Amhurst, 1721 and 1726] (Newark, University of Delaware Press, 2004)
Robinson 1882	C. J. Robinson, *Register of the Scholars Admitted into Merchant Taylors School, from A.D. 1562 to 1874* (2 vols. Lewes, 1882–3)
Salter 1912	H. E. Salter, *Survey of Oxford in 1772* (Oxford, 1912)
Salter 1923	H. E. Salter (ed.), *Surveys and Tokens* (OHS lxxv, 1923)
Salter 1926	H. E. Salter, *Oxford City Properties* (Oxford, 1926)

Screech 1997	M. A. Screech, H. H. E. Craster, and F. E. Hutchinson, *Monumental Inscriptions in All Souls College* (2nd edn. Oxford, 1997)
Shadwell 1902	C. L. Shadwell, *Registrum Orielense*, vol. 2 (1701–1900) (London, 1902)
Sharpe 2004	J. A. Sharpe, *Dick Turpin, The Myth of the English Highwayman* (London, 2004)
Sillery 1990	*St. John's College Biographical Register, 1660–1775* compiled by V. Sillery (Oxford, printed for private circulation, 1990)
Sinclair & Robb-Smith 1950	H. M. Sinclair and A. H. T. Robb-Smith, *A Short History of Anatomical Teaching in Oxford* (Oxford, 1950)
Skelton 1823	J. Skelton, *Oxonia Antiqua Restaurata* (2 vols. Oxford, 1823)
Smart 1750	C. Smart, *The Student, or, the Oxford and Cambridge Monthly Miscellany* (2 vols. London, Oxford, and Cambridge, 1750–1)
Smith 1978	E. H. F. Smith, *St Peter's: The Founding of an Oxford College* (Gerrard's Cross, 1978)
Sparrow 1960	J. Sparrow, 'An Oxford Altar-piece', *Burlington Magazine* 102, no. 682 (1960), 4–9, and no. 691 (1960), 452–3, 455
Sparrow 1965	J. Sparrow, 'Mengs's All Souls altar-piece: a further note', *Burlington Magazine* 107, no. 753 (1965), 631–2
Spokes 1964	P. S. Spokes, *Summary Catalogue of Manuscripts in the Bodleian Library relating to the City, County and University of Oxford: Accessions from 1916 to 1962* (Oxford, 1964)
Stainer 1901	C. L. Stainer, *Studies on Oxford History, Chiefly in the Eighteenth Century* (OHS xli, 1901)
Stephens 1883	F. G. Stephens, *Catalogue of Prints and Drawings in the British Museum*, Division

I: political and personal satires (London, 1883)

Sutherland & Mitchell 1986 — L. S. Sutherland and L. G. Mitchell (eds.), *History of the University of Oxford*, vol. 5: *The Eighteenth Century* (Oxford, 1986)

Taunt 1905 — H. W. Taunt, *The Boar's Head at Queens College Oxford* (2nd edn. Oxford, [1905])

Terrae-Filius — See above, Amhurst, 1726, 1733

Thiselton-Dyer 1900 — T. F. Thiselton-Dyer, *British Popular Customs, Present and Past* (London, 1900)

Tyack 1998 — G. Tyack, *Oxford: An Architectural Guide* (Oxford, 1998)

Tyacke 1997 — N. Tyacke (ed.), *History of the University of Oxford*, vol. 4: *Seventeenth-Century Oxford* (Oxford, 1997)

Ward Jones & Burrows 2002 — P. Ward Jones and D. Burrows, 'An inventory of mid-eighteenth-century Oxford musical hands', *Royal Musical Association Research Chronicle*, vol. 35 (2002), 61–139

Warren 1907 — T. H. Warren, *Magdalen College, Oxford* (London, 1907)

Welch 1852 — J. Welch, *List of the Queen's Scholars of St. Peter's College, Westminster* (new edn. London, 1852)

Wells 1898 — J. Wells, *Wadham College* (London, 1898)

West Wales Hist. Rec. — *West Wales Historical Records*: annual magazine of the Historical Society of West Wales, ed. F. Green (14 vols. Carmarthen, 1912–29)

Wilson 1922 — G. D. A. F. Wilson, *Letters to Somebody: A Retrospect* (London, 1922)

Wilson 1924 — W. H. B. J. Wilson, *Green Peas at Christmas*: *Hunting Reminiscences* (London, 1924)

Wilson 1970 — F. P. Wilson (ed.), *Oxford Dictionary of English Proverbs* (3rd edn. Oxford, 1970)

Wollenberg 1981 Susan Wollenberg, 'Music in 18th-century Oxford' in *Proceedings of the Royal Musical Association*, vol. 108 (1981/2), 69–99

Wollenberg 2001 Susan Wollenberg, *Music at Oxford in the Eighteenth and Nineteenth Centuries* (Oxford; New York, 2001)

Wollenberg & McVeigh 2004 Susan Wollenberg and S. McVeigh (eds.), *Concert Life in Eighteenth-Century Britain* (London, 2004)

Wood, *Hist. Univ.* A. Wood, *History and Antiquities of the University of Oxford*, ed. J. Gutch (3 vols. Oxford, 1786–96)

Wood, *Life* *The Life and Times of Anthony Wood*, ed. A. Clark (5 vols. OHS xix, xxi, xxvi, xxx, xl, 1889–1900)

Woodforde 1951 C. Woodforde, *The Stained Glass of New College, Oxford* (London, 1951)

Wright 1827 J. M. F. Wright, *Alma Mater or, Seven Years at the University of Cambridge by a Trinity-Man* (2 vols. London, 1827)

INDEX

Note: Places are assigned to counties as defined before 1974.